CINDY LORA-RENARD

Foreword by D. Patrick Miller

SPIRITUAL COUPLING

A Guidebook for
Experiencing a Holy Relationship

From Principles of
A COURSE IN MIRACLES

PRAISE FOR
~Spiritual Coupling~

"With her new book, Spiritual Coupling: A Guidebook for Experiencing a Holy Relationship, Cindy Lora-Renard gives us a wonderful and comprehensive examination of most relationships and what it takes to turn them into Holy ones. This book isn't about Cindy and me, although there is a part about me; it's a book for everyone who is either in a relationship or would like to be. I've seen Cindy's knowledge and wisdom grow over the years to the point where she has become one of the finest spiritual teachers and writers in the world. If you're interested in expanding your awareness, don't miss this important book!"

> —**Gary Renard**, the best-selling author of *The Disappearance of the Universe* trilogy, and *The Lifetimes When Jesus and Buddha Knew Each Other.*

"Get your pen ready as you're going to want to take notes! Spiritual Coupling is more than a book. It's a guide on how to bring spiritual principles into your relationships and life. Cindy Lora-Renard combines her expert understanding of *A Course in Miracles* with her gentle nature to help us feel safe to turn within and uncover those pesky blocks to love, which pollute our relationships. I, personally, enjoy that Cindy continuously highlights and reinforces the important and powerful law of the mind – as you see others, you will see and therefore experience yourself. Cindy will help you clearly understand this law, so it becomes your gateway to experiencing compassion, healing, and genuine peace in your relationships, and consequently, within yourself. I'm loving my increased commitment to healing and enjoying my relationships since reading this genuinely helpful guide."

> —**Fiona Williams** - Author of "Awakening Your Right Mind - Healing from Fear and Following Spirit with A Course in Miracles"; Spiritual Coach; CHt; ECPC

"Cindy Lora-Renard has written a beautiful guidebook to support learning in our most important classroom – our relationships. Her book covers a wide range of helpful relationship-related topics, with abundant examples, which draw from her many years of experience as a spiritual counselor and teacher of *A Course in Miracles*. Cindy's teachings are consistent and rooted in love and healing, and she is grounded in the truth that healing our relationships helps us heal our belief in separation from God. No matter your relationship status, you will get so much out of this book!"

   —**Corinne Zupko, Ed.S.**, award-winning and bestselling author of
   From Anxiety To Love

Few books directly address the fundamental aspects of being in a relationship with another person as well as Cindy Lora-Renard's book, Spiritual Coupling: A Guidebook for Experiencing a Holy Relationship. Using *A Course in Miracles* as the foundation, Cindy shares personal life examples in her teaching. She describes the difference between the holy relationship, based on unconditional love, and what passes for love in the physical world, referred to as special relationships. When we learn to forgive our projections onto others' and the world, we enter the sacred space of our existence and catch a glimpse of that reality, which has a positive effect on our relationships. Cindy explains that the Holy relationship is not a romance, is not possessive, nor exclusive, but a transcendent state from appearing to be separate from all there is into being one with everything. What a lovely journey to take with Cindy while reading her book! Again, her metaphors inspire, transcend and revive!

   —**Gabriela Ilie, Ph.D.**, Dalhousie Medical Research
   Foundation Endowed Soillse Scientist in
   Prostate Cancer Quality of Life Research
   Associate Professor

CINDY LORA-RENARD

Foreword by D. Patrick Miller

SPIRITUAL COUPLING

A Guidebook for
Experiencing a Holy Relationship

From Principles of
A COURSE IN MIRACLES

I dedicate this book to all the visible and non-visible teachers who have inspired me to live my best life. I am eternally grateful for their continued support, comfort, and encouragement as I walk the path home to God.

Sometimes you have to close your eyes to truly see what is in front of you.

Cindy Lora-Renard

CONTENTS

FOREWORD

I confess that I can't think of what *A Course in Miracles* teaches us about relationships without an oddly fond memory of Choosy.

'Choosy' is a rhyming pseudonym for a lovely woman I met during a brief, adventurous period of online dating that followed my divorce after fifteen years of marriage. I found her profile on a year-ending December 31, and wrote to her the next morning, startled to receive an almost immediate response. As I soon learned, it wasn't actually a response. In fact, Choosy and I had sent greetings to each other *simultaneously* on that fateful New Year's Day.

It's a miracle, I thought, assuming that the synchronicity augured well for a deep and significant romance. Instead, the following thirty days brought on a parade of awkward encounters and stilted conversations. Choosy mostly wanted to go to the movies, and we did a lot of that. But that left hours in which we had to talk to each other, and after sharing film reviews, we found little common ground.

Choosy claimed to be an atheist who was nonetheless fascinated by ghost-hunting shows on television. That paradox convinced me that she was probably suppressing an inner spiritual life. So I talked to Choosy — at length, I'm afraid — about how my own spiritual path had been initiated by seven years of a serious illness, Chronic Fatigue Syndrome, how that had led to my first encounter with *A Course in Miracles*, and how that sparked the long healing process that followed...
and so on.

I thought this was a sublime between-movies topic. But I noticed that a glazed look came over Choosy's face every time I prattled on about the Course. By the end of the month she'd had enough. On Jan. 31, she unceremoniously dumped me without a word of explanation.

Flash forward two years. I was bounding down the steps after a gym workout and almost ran over Choosy crossing the street, unknowingly heading straight for me. Besides looking startled, she was also pale and unsteady on her feet, obviously exhausted. I couldn't honestly say "you look great!" so I just asked how she was doing. She replied, "Not so good. I've been sick for months and I was diagnosed with Chronic Fatigue Syndrome."

Immediately I expressed my sympathy — I could honestly say I knew what she was going through — and offered to help with any information or insights that might be useful. Still in wide-eyed surprise, Choosy stared at me and said, "Well, it's so interesting to run into you right this moment. I was just seeing my therapist, and he suggested that I might benefit from looking into *A Course in Miracles.*"

After a brief, silent rush of smug vindication, I responded simply, "Oh really?"

Peering at me ever more intently, Choosy then leaned close and whispered, "So can I ask you something I really need to know?"

"Sure," I whispered back, not clear on why we were being secretive. Choosy briefly cast her eyes both ways down the sidewalk before asking, quite earnestly, "Isn't the Course mostly for, like, *crazy people?!*"

I confess that I burst out laughing right in Choosy's face — for two reasons. First, it was now abundantly clear what conclusion she had reached about me that led to the abrupt dumping. Second, she was utterly on target in her characterization of Course students. So I answered, "Yes, you're absolutely right — as long as you understand that the Course says *everyone* is crazy!"

This unforgettable encounter came freshly to mind while I was enjoying a preview of this book on relationships and *A Course in*

Miracles written by Cindy Lora-Renard. That's because so much of what Cindy has to share is what I would call *extraordinary common sense* — that is, what all of us would already know if we hadn't somehow lost our minds and become crazy people.

Ken Wapnick, the legendary Course philosopher, often pointed out that despite its many challenges and overall difficulty, ACIM is not an advanced spiritual path; in fact it's remedial. It's not designed to lead us straight to enlightenment. Instead it's designed to shock us into recognition of the mess that our ego-soaked lives have become, so that we are led to the humble consideration that "there must be another way." And then step by step, lesson by repetitive lesson, it shows us a way out — a way to sanity inspired by a profoundly different point of view than the sad, tragic, and egocentric perspective we have become accustomed to.

Without a doubt, many of us believe that it's our troubled relationships — which the Course identifies as "special" — that have driven us nuts. The first one we experience is usually the relationship with our parents and/or family of origin, but the kind that tries our sanity as adults is what we usually identify as *romantic*. That's the kind of one-on-one relationship in which a new and alluring partner appears, at first, to be the man or woman "of our dreams" — everything we could want in feeling, intelligence, sexuality, taste in films, and so on. This is what ACIM identifies as the "special love" phase.

Unfortunately, special love all too often degenerates over time into boredom, restlessness, discord, alienation, and ultimately divorce in every sense of the word. That's the "special hate" phase — to which most people have no ready response besides resuming their hopeful, hapless search for a "soulmate."

Cindy throws a very useful wrench into this cycle of special relationships by suggesting that we ask ourselves, "Do I want to find my soulmate if I still have a clogged mind, holding thoughts of lack, judgment or fear? To the ego, the answer is yes, because it needs someone or something to project its unconscious guilt on to, and any body will do."

Hence readers should be forewarned that Cindy is not offering a quick and easy guide to finding the love of your life. She does provide a number of Course-inspired thought tools and meditations, some devised with the help of her husband Gary (I've heard of that guy somewhere before) that will speed the reader's progress with essential disciplines of forgiveness, inner abundance, "fearless communication," and more. And in Chapter 10, she takes on the big kahuna of partnership — that is, the tricky, prickly challenge of deciding whether one wants to be "right or happy."

As Cindy relates, "I have seen countless situations where two people were 'at each other's throats,' because each of them was trying to make the other one wrong, getting absolutely nowhere in their communication." For anyone who's been there, done that, Cindy's insights will be especially helpful.

While *A Course in Miracles* is widely viewed as a self-study discipline that many of us tackle alone at first, it is in our relationships that "the rubber meets the road" in terms of realizing its benefits. Thank God and Cindy for this capable and concise yet comprehensive digest of what the Course brings, not just to our understanding of relationships, but to our ongoing transformation in the midst of them. The quest to find a soulmate, if regarded humbly enough, is an opportunity for self-confrontation, inward Self-discovery, and eventually the continuous sharing of genuine happiness. Granted, some may find it aggravating that it's not just a simple matter of being choosy.

D. Patrick Miller is the founder of Fearless Books, the original publisher of **The Disappearance of the Universe** *by Gary Renard, and author of* **Understanding A Course in Miracles**: *The History, Message, and Legacy of a Profound Spiritual Path (Fearless Books, 2nd edition 2021).*

AUTHOR'S NOTE AND ACKNOWLEDGEMENTS

This is a book about relationships, which are the most important things in our lives, even when that is not recognized. Indeed, some of us think we can get away from what A Course in Miracles calls "special" relationships. That brilliant Course, which will be quoted in this book, is a purely non-dualistic thought system that says only God or perfect love is our absolute reality. Since I gave a more thorough introduction of the basic principles of A Course in Miracles in my other three books, I will be focusing mainly on its perspective on relationships, which take the form of special love and special hate, but neither being the unconditional love of God. So how do we experience this total, unconditional love of God? We can use our relationships for a different purpose, which I'll get into.

Although I will always consider myself a student of A Course in Miracles, which I will now refer to simply as the Course, I have taught its principles for over fifteen years. During this time, the most common questions I've been asked are about relationships, more specifically, how to heal them. There is an answer to this question, but it might not be what you think. As we go along, it will be made clear that there is a connection between healing your relationships in this world and the healing of the belief in separation from God.

Some people might think they can escape special relationships, which is impossible. If you were meditating on a mountaintop in Tibet or stranded on a deserted island by yourself, you'd still be in conflict with someone, and it would be you. On top of that you'd have your memories, but if you're living the so-called "normal" life then an important thing to understand is that your special relationships often involve a great deal of pain. This is because there is guilt in the mind over the belief in separation from God, which was projected out and now seen outside of ourselves, in other people. This is exactly where the ego wants it to be. Our function is not to *escape* special relationships, but transform them. This book will show you how to do that.

We are all born into special relationships. It starts with the ones we have with our parents or whoever raised us into adulthood, and even the ones we judge as not having taken the time to be what we would call "good" parents or our "real" parents. That's the way it was set up. What we have forgotten is that we wanted it that way, just the way we wanted all the other relationships in our lives. This might not seem possible, but that's because there is a veil of forgetfulness over the mind. However, as I will discuss in this book, that forgetting doesn't mean you don't have a mind to choose how you view your relationships and thus have the ability to live peacefully and in harmony with yourself and others, no matter what the form of the relationship. You do. You can and will succeed if you just do your part to the best of your ability.

What is the ultimate relationship? The ultimate relationship is the relationship you have with your Source or God. This is because there is nothing else in reality. In Heaven, the word relationship is meaningless, since it implies there is another to be in relation with, when in fact the ultimate state of being is total oneness. Since we believe we are separate from God, we need to heal this sense of separation. Whether we realize it or not, whenever we heal our special relationships here in the world, it is a reflection of the healing of our ultimate relationship with God, remembering we are one with Him. The holy relationship, or forgiven relationship, is one where you recognize in another their innocence and therefore your own. It takes practice to get to a point in a relationship where the other is viewed as nothing less than God. This might frighten some people, and even be cause for attack in the form of staying away from intimacy with another, or even avoiding the person all together. Cultivating a healthy relationship with yourself, also involving forgiveness, is another way to start the process of healing *all* relationships.

The question isn't whether or not to have relationships. That's something that's already been determined, including the exact people and nature of those relationships. The question is *what are they for?* This book will answer that question in no uncertain terms. It will mostly do so within the context of special love relationships, whether between a man and a woman, or a woman and a woman, or a man and a man. Although the focus will be on romantic relationships, at times I will address relationships in general, including the ones we have with children, since they, too, are an important classroom for all of us to learn our lessons of forgiveness. The dynamics of these relationships are the same, even if the form appears to be different. It will eventually be understood that the goal of our individual self is not to just merely become one with another individual self, as in marriage or some other long term commitment, rather it is to become one with God, which we do by recognizing our oneness with others.

It is unrealistic to demand or even expect complete fulfillment and perfection from someone else when we also understand that we are not perfect here on the level of form. Only God's love can fulfill the illusion of lack that the ego made. This book is designed to answer some commonly asked questions from the non-dualistic perspective the Course is teaching on relationships, as well as help inspire you to experience your relationships as peaceful ones. This can lead to a profound experience of intimacy, and ultimately to the healing of the Sonship as a whole. May we all be blessed with the understanding that love can heal the most powerful addiction we all have…the belief in separation from each other and, ultimately, with God.

This book would not be possible without the support of so many loving and caring people who have inspired me to express myself as fully as I can and live my most authentic life. My deepest gratitude goes to the Voice of the Course (Jesus) whose gentle guidance and unconditional love for us all has inspired me beyond my imagination. Also, a profound expression of thanks to the scribe of the Course, Dr. Helen Schucman, for being willing to fulfill her assignment in taking down notes from the Voice so that it could be shared with millions of people. Her colleague and co-scribe, Bill Thetford, also played a pivotal role in bringing the Course to fruition, working with Helen, and inspiring her to keep moving forward with this most beautiful and compelling document.

I want to thank my amazing husband, Gary R. Renard, for his helpful feedback in the writing of this book, but most importantly for his kindness and encouragement, and always reminding me to not take myself too seriously. I also thank him for his own powerful contribution to the Course community and the world in general, expressing the teachings of the Course, along with Arten and Pursah (the Ascended Masters who appear to Gary), in such a light-hearted, yet impactful and unique way. I am grateful we are awakening in God together.

I further want to acknowledge my incredible family and friends for their unconditional love and support. More specifically, I thank my mother, Doris Lora, a Course student and an editor of this book. She truly lives the principles of the Course, being an inspiration to myself and many others. Her loving attention and care in whatever I set out to do mean so much to me. I would also like to thank my father, Ron Lora, for continuing to be an endless source of support and encouragement along my journey, always being willing to listen with an open mind, and show such a genuine interest in my path. More love and gratitude to my sister, Jackie Lora Jones, also a student and teacher of the Course, who is truly an inspiration to me and my soul sister on the path of awakening. I love how we remind each other of the truth, no matter what comes our way in this unpredictable world.

I would also like to give a profound thank you to my brother-in-law, Mark Jones, who so graciously offers a helping hand when needed, in personal ways as well as tech support. His desire to be truly helpful is admirable. In addition, I thank him for keeping the journey of life so interesting and fun by offering his profound and unique insights.

Another big thank you goes to my stepmother, Alice Lora, and stepsister, Leah Ray, for their kindness and always being supportive in whatever I do. I appreciate their openness as well as the discussions we have on life, which are both enjoyable and inspiring. A deep thank you to my stepbrother, Jeff Ray, who passed in 2014 at the young age of 43, with whom I shared a deep bond and who reminded me to follow my passion by his demonstration of following his own.

I'm so grateful to D. Patrick Miller for writing the Foreword for this book, and for his support of both Gary and me. It is very meaningful. I thank Gabriela Ilie, Fiona Williams, and Corinne Zupko for taking time to read and write endorsements for this book. The support I received from each of you is so valuable to me. I would also like to express a deep thank you to Stefan L. L. Van Heester for his important editing contribution and encouragement.

I feel so much gratitude for the late, great Dr. Kenneth Wapnick, the beloved teacher and most prolific writer about A Course in Miracles, who really understood the teachings of Jesus. I have received much inspiration in my study and practice of the Course from both him and his lovely wife, Gloria Wapnick, founders of the *Foundation for A Course in Miracles*.

Last, but not least, a heartfelt thank you to the authorized publisher and copyright holder of A Course in Miracles, *The Foundation for Inner Peace*, for their years of dedication in making the Course available to millions of people around the world.

Cindy Lora-Renard

CHAPTER 1

THE PURPOSE OF
RELATIONSHIPS

*What better purpose could any relationship have than to invite
the Holy Spirit to enter into it and give it His Own great gift of
rejoicing?*[1]

E very day is the most powerful day of your life, because each day you
are given opportunities to choose how you perceive yourself and
others, which has an effect on all your relationships. There are only two
identities we are always choosing between (the Spirit and the body)
and only Spirit or God is real. According to the Course, the body is an
illusion. This dichotomy of Spirit and body, with only Spirit or God
being real is what the Course means by pure non-dualism. Whichever
identity you perceive yourself to be determines the experience you will
have on a daily basis. We will get into this more as we go along, and the
meaning of pure non-dualism will become even more understandable.
You will see how living from the attitude of pure non-dualism will help
you be at peace in your everyday life. It will help you with anything you
have a relationship with, including yourself, others, and the environment in general. You will also see that the mind will be in conflict until

1

you adhere to only one voice, the Voice of the Holy Spirit, which I will be elaborating on as we go along. The purpose of the world, according to the Holy Spirit, is to learn our lessons of forgiveness. Our special relationships are one of the most important areas in which to learn these lessons.

Our relationships with others are also a tool we can use to gauge where we are in our spiritual development. Therefore, the Course says, it is wise to take any opportunity that arises as a challenge and make the most of it. It puts it this way: *Every minute and every second gives you a chance to save yourself. Do not lose these chances, not because they will not return, but because delay of joy is needless.*[2] When we understand that choosing the Holy Spirit's interpretation of our relationships brings us joy, we will choose it more often. The Holy Spirit, which is the Voice for God, is based on a thought system of wholeness, love and forgiveness. It is completely opposite from the ego's thought system, which is based on the idea of separation, which breeds judgment and attack. This is why using your mind to choose between these two thought systems is so important. It will determine the kinds of experiences you have.

All relationships, no matter what the form, are opportunities for growth and learning. We need them while we appear to be in the world as a body, because they show us all of our judgments and forgiveness opportunities that need to be addressed. Regarding the world, the Course says, *It is the witness to your state of mind, the outside picture of an inward condition.*[3] The mind is cause, and the world is the effect, and that includes our physical and psychological selves.

Relationships are also necessary for deletion. What do I mean by this? Well, those of you who study the Course and have read *The Disappearance of the Universe* by my husband, Gary Renard, know that by practicing true forgiveness, the kind that undoes the ego by seeing innocence in another and yourself, ultimately results in your awakening to your true spiritual nature and *the disappearance of the universe.* This is because the universe/world is a dream, having nothing to do with reality. When we learn all our lessons of forgiveness, we don't need to have the experience of incarnating anymore, and we will be back home in God, to the home we've never left. We are always in Spirit, only dreaming we've left.

Just as the Holy Spirit has a purpose for our relationships, the ego does as well. To the ego, our relationships are for the purpose of projecting our unconscious guilt onto others, making others the guilty ones while we retain our innocence. This is separation at its unfortunate best. Relationships will not thrive under these conditions, because the world itself was made so love could not enter into it. If we are identifying with the ego as we interact with someone, there is no way any issue we may be having will be resolved. We need to go beyond the thinking of the ego to the truth that lies beyond the veil, and remember that we have shared interests with each other. Everyone is doing the best they can with the awareness they have at the time, and are making their way back home to God; everyone. Our love needs to be all-inclusive, in order to make any progress in the "great awakening" of the Sonship. Forgiveness is the main tool the Course uses to inspire us to remember the truth of who we are.

In my first three books, I explain the deeper meaning of forgiveness, using examples of how to apply it in your everyday life. Since this book is about relationships, we'll discuss how to practice it within that context. In this way, forgiveness will become more understandable to you as we go along. It is in our relationships with others (some of whom we've shared countless lifetimes), that we are presented with some of the most powerful forgiveness opportunities. As we let go of judgments of ourselves and others, and learn to work in harmony with others, we can literally delete negative karma built up over lifetimes. As it is deleted, so are the lessons that go along with it. This is what the Course means when it talks about how the "miracle" or shift in perception collapses time. Why is this important? **Well, how important is having a peaceful mind to you?** You may find that I will be repeating this question often, and it's for a reason. Jesus, the Voice of the Course, says, *A tranquil mind is not a little gift.*[4] Suffering isn't necessary. The desire to know yourself as you are in truth is a very worthy form of desire. And *Truth is restored to you through your desire, as it was lost to you through your desire for something else.*[5]

Every encounter you have with another, even if it is a stranger, is an opportunity to teach either love or fear. You are constantly teaching every day by your example. The question is: what are you teaching? If you feel fearful, you are teaching fear. If you feel loving, you are teaching love. Whatever you are teaching really boils down to awareness. By paying attention and training the mind to be aware, you will be in a better position to manage yourself and your emotions, and therefore be a teacher of peace, which will have a positive effect on all of your relationships. To train the mind is to practice true forgiveness and see with spiritual sight every day with anything that comes up that disturbs your peace. Training the mind takes continuous practice and focus. Spiritual sight will also be discussed in more depth in later chapters.

Everyone makes mistakes. For example, when you are going down a road, you may eventually realize it's the wrong road. The key is to recognize it when it happens, and choose a different road. This statement is to be applied at the level of the mind. It's just a mistake that needs correction. There is nothing wrong or bad about choosing the wrong road or making a mistake. How long you stay on the wrong road (in the ego mind) depends on how aware you are, as well as having the humility to say, "I was wrong. I was mistaken in my choice (for the ego) and now I bring my mistaken choice to the light of the Holy Spirit." What this means is that we are bringing our illusions to the truth, and accepting the correction (the Atonement) for ourselves, which inspires others to do the same. Atonement in the Course is not the same thing as Atonement in the Bible. Atonement in the Course means undoing the belief in separation, recognizing for oneself that the separation from God has not really occurred, which means we are innocent. We are merely dreaming a dream. This idea is also part of what it means to have an attitude of forgiveness. In other words, we take full responsibility for our perceptions, recognizing what we are seeing isn't true, because it's all made up, being a projection of the mind's belief in separation.

Another key idea to remember while you are practicing forgiveness in your relationships is to remember that forgiveness is done at the level of the mind and has nothing to do with behavior. In fact, forgiveness is not between bodies because it is a correction that occurs in the mind, and it is for your benefit. The miracle or forgiveness is a shift in perception from fear/ego based thinking to love which is inspired by the Holy Spirit. Forgiveness is easier when you realize that it is *you* that you are freeing as a prisoner of your own mind. You may be guided to take some form of action that you feel is necessary, but that action might not feel good to your partner or to whom you are attempting to forgive, and that's okay. The important thing is that it comes from a place of love. The place of love I am referring to is the right part of your mind where your memory of God or the Holy Spirit resides. If you let yourself be guided by the Holy Spirit, your experience will shift for the better, but the outcome of your forgiveness is not your responsibility. You can let the Holy Spirit be in charge of the outcome.

If you are inspired to take some sort of action after you have asked the Holy Spirit for guidance, even if it doesn't make sense to you, you can trust it. You can't always see the bigger picture or what is best as well as the blessings that may come from following your guidance. As long as you do your forgiveness work sincerely, that's all that matters. Since this book is about developing a holy relationship, most of my examples will be within the context of romantic relationships. However, the kind of forgiveness I am talking about is meant to be applied to any relationship or situation you want to forgive. For example, let's say your partner is being very abusive to himself or herself or to you, and it's negatively affecting parts of your relationship such as your health and well-being, or your ability to communicate. The form of the abuse is irrelevant. You may be guided to remove yourself from the situation, whether it's in your home, on the street, in your car, or wherever. You don't have to subject yourself to abuse. You can remove yourself from the violence and practice forgiveness at the same time, or practice forgiveness later when you remember to do it. Even if you find yourself out of character, doing something you wouldn't normally do, remember it's not about behavior. Rather, it's the decision to be loving to yourself and take good care of yourself, which ultimately serves the whole. **When one heals, we all heal**.

If things seem unmanageable for the majority of the time, affecting your ability to live with comfort, no matter what you do, it is also a sign that you may want to pay attention to what your inner guidance is telling you. You will know by how you feel. If you aren't ready to address your partner, you can be sure the time will come when there will be no doubt about what you should do. Forgiveness will lead the way and open doors that have remained closed for a long time. A question you could ask yourself in challenging moments is: What do I want to come of this? What is the most loving thing I can do right now? Or, what is the most loving thought I can hold right now? This will put you immediately back on the path to love. You can't be helpful to yourself or another if you are not in peace, but are in a state of fear. The point is to use whatever situation you find yourself in as an opportunity for forgiveness, and then act accordingly. Remember, too, that when the ego senses "change" coming it will do its job, which is viciously "attack" you in whatever way it can, because its identity is being threatened. As the Course says, and this will be repeated again later, *The ego is therefore capable of suspiciousness at best and viciousness at worst. That is its range.*[6] When you have identified with the ego, believing it is *you*, then you will feel fear. There is a way out of this, and this will be discussed (with examples) as we go along.

Another important idea is to focus on your *own* forgiveness lessons, not somebody else's. The best example you can set for others is being in a state of joy, defenselessness, and peace, no matter what is going on around you. This takes a lot of practice. You don't have to be perfect, but you can do your best to stay connected to Source/ God. This will raise your vibration so that you don't feel entangled in conflict. If your partner is doing something that annoys you, after you practice forgiveness, practice not allowing your mind to dwell on what you think he or she did, but remember there is another way of looking at it. Live your life anyway, doing things that you enjoy. Surround yourself with positive people, play with your pet, take a walk in nature, and just continue on with your life to the best of your ability. Have you heard the saying "Dance like no one else is watching"? In other words, be your authentic Self.

You don't have to stop your life because your partner is not living up to your expectations. You may want to practice not assigning a role to your partner that you would have them fulfill. That is not your job. You can be interested and engaged with your partner, which is normal, but I assure you that if you practice living your life without *attachment* to what your partner is doing, it will be a relationship with much less suffering. This doesn't mean that you condone abusive behavior or tolerate something that is not healthy for you, or pretend that nothing matters and that you don't care. It only requires that you shift how you are looking at it, and then take whatever action seems necessary from that place of healthy perspective and inner balance.

WHAT ARE SOULMATES?

One of the most commonly asked questions we receive at our workshops is from people who are single and who would like a life-long partner. The question is: "Who is my soulmate?" Or, "How do I find my soulmate?" Soulmates seem like a very romantic idea, because we have interpreted it to mean that we will meet that "special" person who will satisfy all our imagined needs. In other words, that person, we hope, will complete us. Even if you feel you have found your soulmate, there will still be lessons to be learned. Also, who says a soulmate has to be a romantic partner? Perhaps a soulmate can be anyone with whom you have the potential to make of it a holy relationship. In other words, all relationships in the world are special, or based on *conditional* love, until we shift their purpose so they serve the Holy Spirit, in which they become holy relationships.

The Course says the script is written. It also says, *There are no accidents in salvation. Those who are to meet will meet, because together they have the potential for a holy relationship. They are ready for each other.*[7] In those terms, how could you *not* find your soulmate if you accept that definition? If it is in your script, you will meet the person you are supposed to meet, so you can learn your lessons of forgiveness, which, again, is the whole point of relationships. With this perspective, there is no need to worry.

To repeat, forgiveness is letting go of the idea of separation (an illusion) which has been projected onto another person or the world, and instead recognizing that nothing happened. This means you and everyone else are innocent, still whole in God's love. The problem most people have with forgiveness is that they think they are forgiving the truth instead of illusions. So, they make the error real first, *then* attempt to forgive it. This is the ego's way of keeping the separation in place.

In the Gospel of Thomas, saying 22, Jesus says: *When you make the two into one, and when you make the inner like the outer and the outer like the inner, and the upper like the lower, and when you make male and female into a single one, so the male will not be male and the female will not be female...then you will enter the Kingdom.* In other words, when you let go of making the other person different from you, which is to make them and yourself separate, and instead see your shared interests with another, you are preparing your mind to enter the Kingdom of Heaven. The Kingdom of Heaven is an awareness of perfect oneness, and a state of true peace.

The Course also says, *As you see him you will see yourself. As you treat him you will treat yourself. As you think of him you will think of yourself. Never forget this, for in him you will find yourself or lose yourself.*[8] You can use your relationships to recognize your innocence, and not lose your Spirit. Since there is only one Mind, anything you think about another person is really what you believe to be true about yourself. This doesn't mean you will always agree with people or what they are doing. It pertains to the way you think. If you think of someone as unworthy of forgiveness, then you are making a statement that *you* are unworthy of forgiveness. If you say you hate another person, you really hate yourself. The way you think about other people plays a huge role in forgiveness. When you start to realize that all minds are joined, you wouldn't want to project your unconscious guilt onto others, because you would know it's really hurting yourself. Understanding how the mind works is very helpful in navigating through very difficult interactions with people.

Coming back to soulmates, in my experience, most people who have found their soulmate, met the person when they were *not* looking. This is what happened to Gary and me. In fact, after I got divorced from my first husband, the last thing on my mind was getting into another relationship and getting married again. I didn't even think I wanted to be married again. In other words, I wasn't looking for anyone. This way, the process of our relationship unfolded naturally.

One thing to keep in mind if you are single is to watch for the ego's judgment that says, "Something is wrong with me because I don't have a partner." If you find yourself saying this regularly, work on loving yourself unconditionally, as God Loves you, regardless of whatever traits you don't like about yourself. As a metaphor, the Course expresses the idea that you are so worthy that God Himself is incomplete without you. I'll repeat this later, because it is worth reinforcing. When you cultivate unconditional love for yourself, you are not only doing yourself a great service, but you are preparing yourself for meeting a possible partner, coming from abundance in your mind, not lack. Also, who says that you have to stop extending your love just because it's not in the form of a romantic partner? Love is love, and it's a trick of the ego when you hear a voice saying "I must not be loving or even capable of loving if I don't have a romantic partner." Extend love wherever you go, and you will experience it within yourself.

We will come back to the idea of abundance being in the mind in a later chapter. For now, a key point is to understand that you can be at peace regardless of your relationship status. This happens over time, through the practice of forgiveness. Perhaps you find yourself annoyed or even upset that you have not found your soulmate. A question to ponder is…do I want to find my soulmate if I still have a clogged mind, holding thoughts of lack, judgment or fear? To the ego, the answer is yes, because it needs someone or something to project its unconscious guilt on to, and any body will do. The unconscious guilt comes from the idea we really separated from God, and that we attacked Him and threw His love away. That idea, which is buried in the mind, gets projected out in the form of our feeling unfairly treated by others or the world in general. This is why it is very important to resolve your "stuff," and heal any unresolved issues in your own mind the best you can *before* you enter a new relationship. Anything left unhealed will make itself known to you in any relationship. The blessing in that is that it gives you an opportunity to understand what it is you most need to forgive.

At the start of a new relationship, most people experience the feeling that everything is wonderful, loving, full of hope, romantic, and sexually exciting. Then, what happens is that the unconscious guilt creeps up, and usually both partners end up projecting that guilt onto the other. It's not because these are new issues. Those issues were already there or else they wouldn't have come up in the first place. This is why other people aren't the cause of your upset. It was already buried in the unconscious mind, and needed a trigger of some kind to emerge. The point I am making is that this will help you before you enter a new relationship, or find your soulmate, because you are beginning to understand how important it is to take full responsibility for your own healing.

Another point to keep in mind is that just because you think someone may be your soulmate, it doesn't necessarily mean that you are meant to be in a life-long romantic partnership with that person. Most people think of soulmates as those that are meant to be our romantic partners for life, and we collectively believe that is what a soulmate means. I believe a wiser and perhaps more peaceful approach would be to let go of any attachment to defining things your own way (with the ego as your teacher) and trust that whoever you are supposed to be with will appear in Divine timing, and therefore you don't have to seek out that person. Just let it unfold naturally the way it was meant to happen. As you are meeting people, just be aware if you feel a little extra twinge of excitement or a feeling that there is something you can't put your finger on about that person, or maybe they are familiar to you. Whatever it is, pay attention, and then if you feel guided to get to know that person, see if he/she is open to it. Also, remember that there is a reason why we are attracted to certain people. There is most likely something to learn from the other, which can serve the Holy Spirit's purpose. The ego always has its own purpose, and that is to find in others what we feel is lacking in ourselves. This is why we say "You complete me." In truth, you don't need anyone to complete you, as you were created whole.

Before Gary and I met, we were both on the verge of separating from our spouses, and on our way to divorce. As I mentioned, I certainly wasn't looking for someone else to fill the shoes of my former spouse at that time. In fact, I liked the idea of being a single woman and the feeling of freedom that went along with that. I didn't expect what was about to happen the day I met Gary and what would happen next. I wasn't seeking a new relationship, and the last thing I thought would happen was meeting someone very soon and getting married again. This is what I mean by the idea that if it's meant to be, it is meant to be. We met because it was in our script, just as it was in our script to fall in love and work together and create a life together. We were just playing our roles. So, if you find yourself feeling guilty or judging yourself because you haven't found the "right" person, you can trust that it will happen if that is the script you designed. There are no encounters by "chance."

When continuing to ask yourself the question of how to recognize if someone is your life partner, or even how to know whether the one you are already with is your life partner, the following questions may be helpful in gaining some clarity: How do you feel? Do you feel a sense of connectedness or recognition, a sense that this person has a deeper history with you that is beyond this present lifetime, or beyond this world? Do you feel you have an assignment together, work to do in partnership, unresolved material where you are being given an opportunity to come together to resolve and heal it once and for all? Are you more committed to this person and to your growth in a way you haven't felt before? Keep in mind as I said earlier, even if you say yes to all these questions, it doesn't necessarily mean you will be with this person for your life term, but you might be if that is your script.

The Course talks about three levels of relationships: A level one relationship is a very brief encounter with someone, where you are given an opportunity to make that a holy relationship. It could be someone you meet in an elevator. Perhaps for one instant you didn't judge the person, but you smiled at the person, and joined in your mind with them, not knowing how much that smile meant to that person. That is a holy encounter. It is an opportunity to join with another with a common goal, to acknowledge the Divinity in each other as one. These encounters are usually brief, and most likely you won't see that person again.

A level two relationship is a more intense, longer lasting relationship such as in marriage or with friends, or even family members, but doesn't necessarily mean you will be in a relationship with them your entire life. Usually it will last as long as it needs to, that is, once they have learned all they can learn from each other at that point in time.

A level three relationship is life-long, either in marriage, or with a family member or friends. In this relationship the people are ready for each other, and the learning curve is actually perfect. In a level three relationship, if you are married, you may get divorced, but stay connected for the rest of your lives, and therefore it is still a life-long relationship. All of these types of relationships are for the purpose of the relationship becoming holy.

The purpose of knowing about these levels is to understand that any relationship is important in the sense that it is an opportunity to practice being what you really are, which is love. It is also about setting aside differences with the understanding that you have shared interests with others, and that you are the same because you share the same mind. No matter what the form of your relationship, the purpose is to accept it and use it for the Holy Spirit's purpose, *For when you have accepted it with gladness, you will realize that your relationship is a reflection of the union of the Creator and His Son.*[9] We are all God's Son as one.

Something to consider if you find yourself wanting to go out and seek out that special person, wondering if you are going to find them, ask yourself what the purpose is for wanting to find them. What is your goal? Jesus also says in the Course, *The clarification of the goal belongs at the beginning, for it is this which will determine the outcome.*[10] What is your intention? Most of the time, our good intentions are not enough because they are ego motivated. It is wiser to look at what part of the mind the motivation is coming from. In other words, motivation is usually of the ego, whereas inspiration is from the Holy Spirit. If you are motivated by the ego to seek out a soulmate, you will recognize it by a feeling of lack that you are trying to fulfill. This can also take the form of not feeling whole when you are alone. What is happening here is that the ego is being sneaky, and unconsciously wants to find another body so that it can project all its unconscious guilt onto it. That is the ego's purpose for relationships. If you are feeling inspired or guided from a loving place, your purpose will be different. It will come from a place of wanting to share and join with another for the purpose of learning and growth, that is, you will already feel abundant in your mind, and therefore want to share that joy with another. It won't be about getting something from another that you feel you lack within you, which is what the special relationship is all about.

Usually, when you are coming from a place of feeling abundant, things unfold naturally, without any effort. There is a sense of freedom in that, not being at the effect of the world and what does or does not happen in the world. You will remain at cause, where you get to decide how you think and feel. That is real power; your power to choose the ego as your teacher or the Holy Spirit. There is such a thing as attractive qualities, and I assure you that if you are exuding the qualities of wholeness, abundance, confidence, and joy, you will be a magnet to others, because people are drawn to the light. What all of us are really seeking is our connection with our Source/God, and, unbeknownst to most people, the ego uses its special relationships as a substitute for God's love. It is God's love that we are seeking, although we only need to awaken to the idea that we are already perfect love and at home with God.

Gary and I know someone who thought of committing suicide, because a woman he loved decided to be with someone else. He said he was suffering and felt a deep loss. For starters, if you or someone you know is having suicidal thoughts, please know there is help available and please do what you can to talk to someone about it. You don't have to go through those feelings alone. In my second book, *The Business of Forgiveness*, I devoted a whole chapter to depression and suicide, which may be helpful to someone experiencing these feelings. When you are completely identified with the ego, it produces all kinds of feelings that come from the emotion of fear. When you begin to realize that your real identity has nothing to do with this world and your body, or other bodies, you will start to feel more empowered as Spirit. You are a decision-making mind that has the power to choose *how* you interpret anything that appears to happen in your script. You might not have control over what happens, but you do have control over how you think. No outside source has the power to control you or make you feel a certain way unless you give it that power.

Most of us feel lonely at times, but it may be helpful to look at what loneliness is really saying to us. It says: *I am different than my Creator, and I am NOT as God created me. I am a separate and individual self, completely cut off from love, and in feeling this way I get to reaffirm that I exist as an ego, apart from God.* Of course, this couldn't be further from the truth, but the ego, who has a voice of its own, wants you to feel this way so it can remain a victim, keeping the idea that you have a mind apart from you. It wants you to forget that you can return to this mind and choose again, choose another interpretation, remembering the strength of Christ within you, and investing in the Holy Spirit as your teacher. The Holy Spirit *is* your strength because it only knows the Spirit as you, which is whole, innocent, and perfect. Practice investing your faith in this strength, and you will soar in life and in all your relationships!

There is a section in the Course called *Healing and Faith*.[11] This section is both inspiring and important in regards to our relationships. First, what I'd like to do is review what it means to have faith. Having faith is really equated with trusting in something beyond oneself. This means trusting beyond your ego self (the body and personality). In a sense, you trust that there's another part of your mind, the right part of your mind. This part of the mind is operating consistently, so it's constantly streaming through you. The only thing that blocks that voice is our desire to hear another voice. When the Course talks about having faith, it also says that we need to have faith to attain the goal of the Course, which is the attainment of true peace.

The Course is asking us to be vigilant only for God. This is a theme that runs continuously throughout it. It's part of what having faith means; faith that you're beyond the body, and that there is a reality that continues without interruption despite what it seems like in the world of duality. The more we practice having faith in our everyday lives, the more our relationships will improve. When you are in the presence of someone whose mind is healed, you can either accept or reject the offering of that vibration. Sometimes the ego is too afraid to be in a higher vibration because it means the end of the ego. In other words, when we choose the light, the darkness disappears. Imagine being in the heat of an argument with someone and then you remember the truth. You start to change your mind. You are offering another interpretation for the other person the instant you do that. This could stop an argument, cold turkey!

What we can trust is that when we go beyond the body to the decision-making mind and choose the Holy Spirit as our teacher, we will be joining with the thought system of peace, innocence, love and forgiveness. This choice will have benefits beyond what you can imagine in any relationship you are having with someone. There is a line in the Course that says, *We said before that when a situation has been dedicated wholly to truth, peace is inevitable.*[12] This is about having willingness and motivation. We have to have the willingness to really want the peace of God above all else. Jesus also says…*peace without faith will never be attained, for what is dedicated to truth as its only goal is brought to truth by faith.*[13]

Think of a relationship right now in your life that challenges you or feels upsetting. Imagine having faith that even though in this moment it might not look like a pretty picture, having faith is going beyond that to what we can't see. We can't see the bigger picture, but how do we know something huge and wonderful isn't around the corner? Martin Luther King Jr. said, "Faith is taking the first step even when you don't see the whole staircase." The Course would say, faith is taking the first step on the ladder (the ladder that the ego led us down) without seeing the whole ladder, yet choosing the Holy Spirit as our teacher when we take that step. We don't have to see the whole picture. It is helpful to know in our minds that there is a bigger picture going on, but we're only asked to take it one step at a time. Try to keep your challenges in that context, that as long as you just keep moving right up the ladder, step by step, through forgiving whatever's right in front of your face on any given day, you might not feel so overwhelmed. Often, we want to get to the end goal, but the end doesn't matter because the ending is that you've succeeded. You cannot fail, because the world is over. It's only about accepting the Atonement for oneself, to repeat an important point. You are going to get there regardless of what happens in your script.

Our whole experience in the world is based on the idea that we've sinned. Unconsciously, we believe so strongly that we've sinned, that we base our reality on that idea. The Course says:

> It is essential that error be not confused with sin, and it is this distinction that makes salvation possible. For error can be corrected, and the wrong made right. But sin, were it possible, would be irreversible. The belief in sin is necessarily based on the firm conviction that minds, not bodies, can attack. And thus the mind is guilty, and will forever so remain unless a mind not part of it can give it absolution. Sin calls for punishment as error for correction, and the belief that punishment is correction is clearly insane.[14]

> Sin is not an error, for sin entails an arrogance which the idea of error lacks. To sin would be to violate reality, and to succeed. Sin is the proclamation that attack is real and guilt is justified. It assumes the Son of God is guilty, and has thus succeeded in losing his innocence and making himself what God created not.[15]

The following statement is the one mistake we all tend to make when it comes to true forgiveness: *Any mistake can be corrected, if truth be left to judge it. But if the mistake is given the status of truth, to what can it be brought?*[16] This is really important because most of us equate our mistakes with truth. That's why it's so hard to forgive, because we're making mistakes, or our illusions, reality. True forgiveness is forgiving our illusions, not forgiving reality. We can bring our mistakes to the Holy Spirit's right-minded perception of love, innocence, and wholeness, through the process of forgiveness. Forgiveness *is* healing.

The Course says sin has become holy *because* we've made it real. What is truly holy is forgiving the *secret sins and hidden hates*[17] that we see in other people, but are only a belief in our own minds. This is an important part of forgiveness. What we want to have faith in is the idea that mistakes can be corrected, and sin is impossible. Sin is just a belief, and beliefs can be changed. When the Course talks about mistakes, it means our mistaken thoughts, thinking with the ego as well as the grievances and judgments we're holding about ourselves and others. When we let these go, we are free!

It's wonderful to have faith that you're not a body. Nevertheless, it is important to take care of yourself at the same time. Remember, the Course says, *To have faith is to heal. It is the sign that you have accepted the Atonement for yourself, and would therefore share it. By faith, you offer the gift of freedom from the past, which you received. You do not use anything your brother has done before to condemn him now. You freely choose to overlook his errors, looking past all barriers between yourself and him, and seeing them as one.*[18] Every time we find ourselves in a situation where we can't forgive someone for something, we can remember that having faith means we are healing; or making whole. The practice becomes not seeing other people as separate from us. At the level of the mind, there's no gap. There appears to be gaps between bodies, but that's an illusion. Any moment that you feel you are losing faith, and even losing faith in yourself to forgive, remember this: The mind is the projector projecting out billions of bodies, but there's only one projector or one mind, which means all the bodies that you appear to see are part of the greater mind. The bodies on the screen all believe they're separate minds, because that's our experience. It's also a trick.

Every time we don't forgive someone, it's being unkind to ourselves. We're saying we aren't worthy of forgiveness if we don't think other people are worthy. Through the eyes of faith, the Son of God is seen as forgiven, whole and healed. We're free of all the guilt that we laid upon ourselves.

As I've been observing the world over many years, I have come to the realization that *what the world needs now is love,* as the popular song states, written by Hal David; music composed by Burt Bacharach. The problem is not that we can't awaken to love, but that the world wasn't made with love. This means we need to choose love and forgiveness, and find peace within ourselves first before we can experience love in the world. If there is no inner peace, there will be no outer peace as a reflection. When you look in a mirror, you see your reflection. If you are smiling, the mirror will show it. If you are frowning, it will also show that. The mirror (the reflection) cannot give you back what you aren't putting out. On a macro scale, the Course says, *Projection makes perception. The world you see is what you gave it, nothing more than that. But though it is no more than that, it is not less. Therefore, to you it is important. It is the witness to your state of mind, the outside picture of an inward condition.*[19]

RAISING CHILDREN TO BECOME HEALTHY ADULTS

Since our relationships with children offer some of the most important forgiveness work, I'd like to discuss how one can relate to children and raise them to be healthy adults. One might ask, "Why does it matter what happens in an illusory world or how we raise children?" It matters because almost everyone here believes they are in a body living in a world of time and space. In other words, we all believe we have separated from God, even if it's unconscious to us. As long as this belief exists, it's helpful to be normal in the world, doing things that will help us awaken from the dream of separation.

In the workshops that I do with my husband, Gary Renard, we get a lot of questions about how to teach children the Course. We always say the same thing: "The Course is not written for children, and it's wise to allow a child to have a normal childhood as they are developing and learning to survive in this world. If a child is naturally asking questions about the nature of God or his/her existence and clearly wants to learn more, than you can use discernment with the help of the Holy Spirit as to how to approach these subjects. Perhaps one day when the child is old enough, maybe in high school or college, you can share more ideas or even give them a copy of the Course, but only if they are interested. It won't be helpful to insist they study it. They may have a different spiritual path they want to follow, and you can be certain their script will provide for them whatever is relevant for them to learn."

In regards to children, there are definitely ways in which to raise them so that they develop into healthy adults. Although I'm not a parent in this lifetime, I've certainly had my share of parenting in other illusory lifetimes. I've also observed and interacted with many children over the years during my travels, counseling sessions, and in life in general. The tips below only represent some of the ways you can have a positive influence on a child's developmental process. There are certainly other ways as well. I hope you find these to be truly helpful:

1. Create a safe space in which children can learn from their mistakes without the need to project their feelings onto other people.
2. Teach them that they are powerful enough to have what they need without harming others to get it.

3. Praise them, using positive reinforcement when they do good deeds, or when they behave in ways that come from their intuition or inspired guidance.

4. Teach them things by using what they love or are naturally interested in, instead of diminishing their passions in order for them to learn a lesson.

5. Have open, honest, and clear communication by being a demonstration yourself of one who is in touch with your own emotions and expressing them in ways that aren't being projected onto other people. The Course says, *To teach is to demonstrate. There are only two thought systems, and you demonstrate that you believe one or the other is true all the time. From your demonstration others learn, and so do you.*[20] Children will remember your kind acts or behaviors more than specific words you say to them. It's wonderful to say "I love you," but it's the demonstration of your love that will mean the most.

6. Allow children to develop their natural abilities or whatever it is they are naturally drawn to, giving them the space and time to do so without interfering. Many times a parent will project onto their children a career they wish they would have had, and they now want their children to live out their dreams for them. This behavior can be very controlling, even if it's well-intentioned. Children need time to figure out what direction they want to go in without the obtrusive direction of the parent. Parents can guide and assist in a loving and supportive way, but try and watch the temptation of moving into control. The child's intuition will guide them along their path if you don't interfere too much.

7. Try not to worry so much about the specifics of what your child's future might look like. They will pick up on it and feel threatened or scared, and start feeling insecure. Instead, teach them by your example how much you trust them and their path to unfold in an inspired, healthy, exciting way! This will help

keep your child on a path toward creativity, fun and produc-tivity in a natural way. I remember my parents doing this with me. Neither my mother nor my father insisted I do anything in particular. They just observed what my natural talents were and encouraged me to follow them, but without judgment or control, doubt or worry. This helped me develop my talents in a way that enhanced my abilities naturally.

8. Finally, pay attention to signs that your child might be in trouble or struggling with something. If you really know your child's normal habits, you will most likely be able to tell if something is "off." Sometimes you won't be able to tell, as children can be very good at hiding their true feelings. Just do the best you can to check in and let them know they are unconditionally loved and supported. That's all you can do. Your job isn't to judge your child, just love them. What they ultimately choose to do with their lives (when they become adults) is none of your business. Sometimes you might have to watch your chil-dren make mistakes, even if they seem destructive. You can do what you can to help, but if you find yourself getting attached and too caught up in the specifics and start to feel helpless, it's a sign that you may have become too identified with their per-sonal path and aren't trusting in their ability to choose. This doesn't mean you don't care about them or that you don't try to get professional help, if needed. Stay tuned in and engaged, but you can do so without being over-bearing. There is wis-dom in knowing when it's time to step away from picking up the pieces after your child, which is often not helpful. As an example, The Holy Spirit doesn't diminish the power of our minds to choose by choosing for us. It can guide and assist whenever helpful, but the choice is ours.

The use of fairytales is another wonderful way to teach children the ups and downs of life. Many traditional fairytales show duality, which teaches them that not everything will always go perfectly in the world, but often fairytales will have a solution as well. When children are old enough to understand, you can always introduce the purely non-dualistic nature of God and His love. You can demonstrate that concept from the moment they are born by living it yourself. In other words, you do your best to love them unconditionally. Children need the symbols of the world to grow up to be healthy adults. We all need them because we believe we are here.

Many people who study the Course ask me if they should have children since they don't know if it's in alignment with the Course; bringing in more bodies to a world that doesn't exist. My answer is always the same: The Course addresses the level of the mind, not behavior. There are no rules as to how one should live one's life. There is no moral code of ethics. You can live your life normally and practice the Course at the level of the mind. If you want to have children, then have children. If you want to get married, get married. If you want a certain career, work towards that career. These are all wonderful classrooms in which to learn lessons of forgiveness. There is nothing in the Course that talks about whether or not to have children. Always ask the Holy Spirit for guidance when it comes to your personal life.

Now that you have some background on the purpose of relationships, both from the Holy Spirit's perspective and the ego's, we can move forward on the journey to understanding what it means to exercise our true power of decision, and we can do that in the present moment, which extends forever.

PAGE FOR PERSONAL NOTES

CHAPTER 2

THE POWER OF THE PRESENT

*Time is inconceivable without change, yet holiness does not change.[1]
For what is time without a past and future? It has taken time to
misguide you so completely, but it takes no time at all to be what
you are.[2] Take this very instant, now, and think of it as all there is of
time.[3] To learn to separate out this single second, and to experience it
as timeless, is to begin to experience yourself as not separate.[4]*

The only time we have is *now*, the eternal present. If this is true, then every thought we have, whether a memory that seems to be from the past, or even a thought about the future, is being experienced as if it's happening *now*. Real love, as opposed to the special love of the ego, can only be present and experienced when the mind is free from past and future associations. Real love is all-encompassing and doesn't exclude anyone or anything. This kind of love accepts everyone as the same, equal in worth, and without differences. It sees everyone as perfect Spirit, nothing less than God. It has absolutely nothing to do with romantic love. Obviously, no one can love everyone romantically and be expected to have that kind of a relationship with everyone they meet. The point is that you don't exclude anyone from the all-encompassing

25

love that is unconditional. Real love is not of this world because this world was not made by love. This world is a projection of fear and separation, and does not exist in reality. There is no world, only a belief in the world. The idea of real love is that you love because that is what you are. It is not limited in any way. Love is just itself and doesn't have to do anything to be itself.

Most people have experienced relationships that were extremely difficult, challenging, and hurtful, and some may currently be experiencing this now. When practicing true forgiveness, you can forgive a memory just the same as if you are forgiving something that seems to occur in the present. This is possible because, as I said before, when you have a memory, it is still being re-experienced as if it were happening *now*. So, practicing forgiveness with a memory frees you from the past so you can experience love in the present. To re-state an important point, real power is remembering that you have a mind that you can return to and make a different choice, if what you are choosing is causing you pain. We may not always have a choice as to *what* happens in our scripts, but we do have a choice as to *how* we choose to perceive it, which sets the stage as to how we *experience* it. Perception is interpretation. We can choose to interpret a situation with the Holy Spirit as our teacher (the right part of our minds that knows the truth of our oneness) or with the ego (the wrong part of the mind that reinforces the thought of separation). Whichever choice we make is what we believe we are in any given moment, because we are identifying with it. We are either an ego, making our choices from an illusory thought system based on sin, guilt and fear, or we are perfect Spirit, whole and innocent. The question is…what are we investing our faith in?

It is important to understand that in our relationships, we see what we want to see. Even if someone appears to attack, judge, or treat us unkindly, this is still the case. We would not recognize others' attacks or judgments if we hadn't first chosen to attack and judge in our own minds. Instead, we would see others' attacks as a call for love. We always attack first in our minds, then project that attack thought out, so we do not have to see it in ourselves, but somewhere outside of us, making our attack seem justified. Now we have someone to blame. The ego says, "It's not my fault. They did it to me. That is why I'm innocent." This is what the ego wants. Unconsciously, the ego wants to see it this way so it can remain a helpless victim or a body that can be hurt, abused and abandoned. This was set up ahead of time as part of a larger script. It's not that people consciously want to be abused. **The ego doesn't want you to know you have a mind that you can return to and choose once again what you would have yourself be; perfect Spirit, or an ego.** This idea cannot be repeated enough. This is the ego's way of absolving itself of any responsibility for what appears to happen.

As I said before, you may not have control in the moment as to what happens, but you always have control as to *how* you are looking at it. Please note, this doesn't mean I am encouraging not speaking up, or not standing up for yourself in the case of any kind of abuse. It only means that you can free yourself from feeling like a prisoner of your own thoughts. We remain victims when we refuse to take responsibility for our own thoughts and how we interpret things. This will keep us in a state of powerlessness. **Knowing you are a mind allows you to choose how you think.**

The cause of our pain and suffering is never because of something that appeared to occur outside of us. It's always a choice made in the mind to identify with guilt, the true cause of all suffering. This belief in guilt always comes back to the false belief we separated from God, which the Course refers to as "sin." In truth, we could never sin, since it's impossible to be separated from perfect love. We do unconsciously believe we've sinned, so this is why we need to learn to forgive that belief.

EXAMPLES OF CHOOSING LOVE
OVER FEAR WHEN COMMUNICATING

Let's use an actual example of how (rather than choosing fear) one can practice using the mind to return to a state of love in a challenging situation. A common experience that people often raise in our workshops is the issue of a partner not spending enough time with him/her. Let's say that you feel this in your relationship, and your partner seems to focus more on his/her work than on you or your family. After you remember that there is really no one "out there," but that everything is a projection coming from your mind, the next step is communicating to your partner how you are feeling without making them responsible for the feeling. Usually, one person makes the other person responsible for how they are feeling and the conversation goes something like this: **Note:** After each sentence, I will state the underlying meaning of what the person is really trying to communicate:

"You never spend time with me anymore, and you seem to be more concerned with your work or your friends." (underlying content: I miss the way we were at the beginning when we were excited to be with each other and the feeling of love I felt when we were connecting. I feel disconnected from love.) "It never used to be this way." (underlying content: I want to feel the way I felt when I first met you.) "You're not even home as often as you used to be. Are you having an affair? Tell me what's going on!" (underlying content: I feel helpless and out of control when I don't know where you are. I feel alone, worthless, and afraid.) Your partner might respond with, "What do you mean I never spend time with you? I'm always here for you! How dare you accuse me of having an affair. You don't appreciate me or anything I do for you. All you care about is yourself." (underlying content: I feel so misunderstood, judged, and hurt. It is painful for me.) These are typical scenarios when both parties are coming from their egos, without thinking before they speak, only reacting to their own projections of fear-based thinking. It is impossible to stay in the present and have your thoughts be inspired by love when you are in ego mode, reacting to another's comments without thinking about what your goal is in that moment. What is the purpose of your communication? What do you want to experience? It would be very helpful to ask the above questions in your mind before you speak.

Understanding the underlying content of your partner's statements will make all the difference in your communication with each other. At the deepest level, what we are really saying when we are hurting is this: "Help me. I've lost God, and I'm separate and alone." Having this understanding of yourself and your loved one whenever you are upset can really shift how you deal with things.

Now, let's look at an example of another way of communicating when you feel hurt, coming from the perspective of one who is connected to his/her right mind:

"I'm feeling a bit disturbed lately because I feel like I have disconnected from love. I seem to be making this feeling be about you not spending enough time with me, and looking to you to fix it; but at the same time I realize that you are not the cause of my upset. I feel confused. I just wanted to share what I was feeling, because it's important for me to communicate with you and have an open and honest relationship. Do you have any thoughts about what I've shared? I'd be open to hearing them." Your partner would most likely respond more positively to your feelings because you didn't make it about him or her. In other words, you took responsibility for how you were feeling. They might respond with something like: "Thank you for sharing how you are feeling. It is important to me. I love you very much, and let's see if we can find a way to spend more time together. Let's keep this conversation going until we both feel some resolution about it." This is one example of what an interaction might look like when two people are coming from their right minds; coming from love, not projecting their fears onto each other.

STEPS FOR COMING BACK TO YOUR CENTER

If you find yourself in a situation like this and your partner is not responding well at all to what you are sharing, because he or she is heavily steeped in their ego state of mind, here are some steps that can help you to stay grounded and get centered again before you proceed any further:

1. When a challenge comes up, acknowledge to yourself which part of you is disturbed (i.e. the ego).
2. Remember that you are never upset for the reason you think. You are really upset because you chose the ego and allowed yourself to disconnect from Source/God, and you are re-playing the separation in your mind.
3. Ask the Holy Spirit to look at it with you. To look with the Holy Spirit means to think about the person or situation with correct perception, with spiritual sight, which is thinking about the person as the Holy Spirit would think about them. The Holy Spirit would think in terms of wholeness, innocence, and see that person as perfect Spirit, over-looking his/her mistakes. Also, remember that if a person is not expressing love, they are calling out for it. Then, the appropriate response would be love and compassion. They are just as fearful as you are, and want peace just as you do. People don't always know how to express their feelings so they become fearful and defensive. If you can recognize this it will save you a lot of heartache.
4. Identify any judgments or assumptions you are making about the person or situation, bringing them to the surface without analyzing them. Just look as an observer.
5. Forgive using a true forgiveness exercise, such as *You are*

Spirit, whole and innocent, all is forgiven and released.[5] Or, (and this is one of my favorites, because it reminds the mind that everything that appears to be outside of us is a projection coming from the mind), *You're not really there. If I think you are guilty or the cause of the problem, and if I made you up, then the imagined guilt and fear must be in me. Since the separation from God never occurred, I forgive "both" of us for what we haven't really done. Now there is only innocence, and I join with the Holy Spirit in peace.*[6]

6. Release, and let go, turning it over to the Holy Spirit, trusting in His strength within you. You are not responsible for how your forgiveness/healing is being received by the other person. The Holy Spirit will take your forgiveness, and when the person is ready to accept it, it will be received.

7. Finally, remember to laugh, not at people, but at the seriousness in which we take things. You can create a new reality each moment for yourself by making light of the situation, which means you don't have to let it affect the peace of God within you. This will help you create the miracle (a shift in your perception) and keep you empowered in the present. What you are laughing at is the *tiny mad idea*[7] the Course talks about, which is the idea that you could be separate from your Source. That is the idea that was taken seriously. So, you are not laughing at someone else's expense, only at the temptation to make the separation real. Remember that you and your partner have shared interests, because you share the same mind. That is why you are the same. You both share the part of the mind that identifies with the ego, and the part that identifies with the Holy Spirit, with a decision-maker that chooses between the two. Sharing is the root of all creation, the sharing of God's love with His one Son. That is real sharing;

the acceptance of oneness.

Practice these steps in times of challenges and you may be surprised at how quickly you can turn everything around in your mind.

In addition to these steps, hold onto your faith that as you turn things over to the Holy Spirit, it is being taken care of. Trust. Be mindful throughout your days, paying attention to which teacher you are choosing in your mind at any given moment. Practice seeing any situation that disturbs your peace as an opportunity to bring healing and resolution to it through forgiveness. Clarify your goal at the beginning of your day. I can't imagine a better goal than experiencing true peace. Jesus says in His Course, *I want the peace of God. To say these words is nothing. But to mean these words is everything. If you could but mean them for just an instant, there would be no further sorrow possible for you in any form; in any place or time.*[8] You demonstrate that you mean you want the peace of God by the practice of forgiveness. Sometimes it doesn't seem like you can choose peace. Yet, if you want it more than anything else, it will be chosen.

Finally, practice letting go of any attachment to knowing what is in you or your partner's best interests. Instead, recognize that you do not know what is in your best interest or another's, and ask the Holy Spirit to be the judge for you. If you are not at peace, you can be sure that you are putting your trust in your own strength, and identifying with the ego's plan for your salvation, which always leads to suffering. When we assume we know what is best for ourselves or others, we stop learning. We can't see the bigger picture, so we need a teacher (the Holy Spirit) that can be that non-judgmental presence in our minds, who will direct our efforts with His Vision instead of our limited vision.

Remember, the power lies within you in this very moment to learn your lessons of forgiveness. Take every memory that hurts, or anything that comes up now as an opportunity to use it for the Holy Spirit's purpose, to bring healing and resolution to it, and remember your innocence. These are the true gifts we give to the Holy Spirit, those things that "hurt" us. **The power of the present is recognizing that whatever thoughts are in your mind, whether it be a thought about now, the past or even future, can be forgiven in this moment, because this moment is where your power *is*.**

COMMON MISTAKES IN RELATIONSHIPS

In my years of experience as a spiritual counselor, I've noticed some common mistakes people make in relationships that, when corrected, will make all the difference in your ability to remain at peace:

1. Blaming another for the cause of your unhappiness
2. Assigning roles to your partner that you think he or she should fulfill
3. Looking for your partner to fill the hole you are feeling inside
4. Making the idea of being a victim real in your mind, which makes the world itself real
5. Taking on another's problem and making it your own
6. Leaving a relationship before you've honored it completely, or before you have taken care of any unfinished business that you might later regret

If you are currently experiencing difficulty in a relationship, you can be sure there is something important there for you to look at, to learn, and bring to resolution and healing. It is something your Soul wants to learn. Even if the other person is not willing to go to that place with you, you can still bring it to healing in your own mind by practicing forgiveness, which the Course says is your only function here. It is also the key to happiness. Action should only be taken if it is inspired and you feel guided. You need do nothing with the ego as your teacher.

To do nothing is to rest, and make a place within you where the activity of the body ceases to demand attention. Into this place the Holy Spirit comes, and there abides.[9] *For from this center will you be directed how to use the body sinlessly.*[10] In other words, you need do nothing (with the body/ego) because the power is in your mind. What you do is return to the mind where you can make a different choice. If, when you choose to do something, it inspires peace within you, you can be sure you are thinking right-mindedly, with the Holy Spirit as your teacher, and you can trust that. But again, what you always do is practice forgiveness, which undoes the guilt in your mind that says you deserve to suffer.

We only have past memories and whatever is happening in the present to draw upon for our consideration. If we consider that past, present, and future are all *one*, then whatever we are thinking in the present is having an influence in all dimensions of time and space. Although time/space is an illusion, it still appears to exist in our experience, so why not make the best choices we can, which can lead us to experience the happy dream of forgiveness while we appear to be here in a body. This happy dream of forgiveness precedes our awakening and is a necessary condition of the mind before re-entering the Kingdom of Heaven, which is a state of perfect oneness, love, and peace. So, there is power in thoughts of the past when we use those thoughts to make the correction in the present, bringing them to the light of truth.

Correction *is* forgiveness. We don't know how to correct ourselves, but when we forgive, the Holy Spirit will do Its part. Let Him handle the results of your forgiveness. This is all about bringing our illusions of separateness to the truth that only love is real; only God exists. That is why the Course says, God Is. There *is* nothing else. Let us not forget the opening lines in the Course: *Nothing real can be threatened. Nothing unreal exists. Herein lies the peace of God.*[11] In other words, what is real is perfect Spirit (God). What is unreal is everything else that seems to be its opposite, and can shift or change, and those things do not exist.

Reciting these lines from the Course is also very helpful when you feel stuck in the past, or stuck in your relationships in general. Having the awareness that our mistaken choice for the ego only calls for correction, not punishment, is a gentle way of helping the ego to be undone, one layer at a time.

When you are going about your day and find yourself running into what you might call strangers, recognize the power you have to use those interactions for the purpose of inspiration, unity, and empathy. Being empathically connected to others is to understand what they might be going through without the need to judge them or join in the pain. You can transfer this learning to include your special love partners. This kind of thinking also keeps you in the present. Judgment is of the past. The first judgment all of us collectively appeared to make is that God is an unjust and punishing God, and therefore we will experience the consequences of our actions. How terrifying to think of a God such as this! Therefore, we can ask ourselves, would the God we pray to want His Sons to be fearful and deserving of punishment? Fortunately, the answer is no. When we accept the power that was given us to create as God creates (in Heaven) we will know our true strength.

The Course says, *The power of the Sons of God is present all the time, because they were created as creators. Their influence on each other is without limit, and must be used for their joint salvation.*[12] As you can see, the best use of our power is to recognize that we can't awaken in God alone. We need our brothers and sisters just as much as they need us so that we will learn what it means to love unconditionally, without limits of any kind. To love one is to love everyone. How twisted our use of power has become! To the world, power is based on how prestigious our jobs are or how much money we have accumulated, and who rules the world. This is a false sense of power and doesn't really exist. In personal relationships, power has been used to intimidate others into doing what we think they should do. If they don't, we don't love them anymore. Welcome to the world of special relationships! Our special love relationships are merely masks over special hate. There are people we choose to love, but since this love is based on conditions, underneath it all is a relationship based on fear, distrust, and competition. Here is what the Course says about our special relationships:

The special relationships of the world are destructive, selfish and child-ishly egocentric. Yet, if given to the Holy Spirit, these relationships can become the holiest things on earth - the miracles that point the way to the return to Heaven. The world uses its special relationships as a final weapon of exclusion and a demonstration of separateness. The Holy Spirit trans-forms them into perfect lessons in forgiveness and in awakening from the dream. Each one is an opportunity to let perceptions be healed and errors corrected. Each one is another chance to forgive oneself by forgiving the other. And each one becomes still another invitation to the Holy Spirit and to the remembrance of God.[13]

As we can see from the above statement, we forgive ourselves by forgiving others, because we are truly joined as one mind. When we choose not to forgive, the relationship becomes destructive in every sense of the word. The question is, what do we truly want? What is most important to us? Would we rather be right or happy? Pondering these questions will bring clarity and a sense of purpose to your rela-tionships that can truly shift your experience of them.

ABOUT GARY AND ME

In my relationship with Gary, I don't intend to paint a perfect picture of it, as if everything goes well all the time. That wouldn't be realistic. There are many wonderful aspects to our relationship, and I am truly grateful to have Gary in my life, as well as the opportunities we have to learn and grow together. There are also times when we disagree on things. **Remember, being in a relationship doesn't mean you will always see eye to eye on things. It's about understanding that you** might disagree at times, but accepting and respecting your part-ner's power to choose the ego or the Holy Spirit. In no way is it helping when we try and take away another's power of decision. You can still make choices as you are guided, while allowing your partner to make his or her choices, too. Sometimes your paths will continue to be aligned and sometimes they won't. Any rela-tionship can work even if there are disagreements. It's only when disagreements turn into violence or abuse of some kind that one needs to pay attention so that those little pebbles of conflict don't become big boulders.

When Gary and I disagree, there might be a slight annoyance, but since both of us know how to forgive, the annoyance doesn't last. We also don't nit-pick each other on the seeming little things, such as which way does one put the toilet paper on the roll. You get the idea. There is tremendous room for growth in both the seeming little disagreements as well as the bigger ones. The Course is teaching us that both our little annoyances and intense rage are really the same, because they obscure the truth. It says:

> Perhaps it will be helpful to remember that no one can be angry at a fact. It is always an interpretation that gives rise to negative emotions, regardless of their seeming justification by what **appears** as facts. Regardless, too, of the intensity of the anger that is aroused. It may be merely slight irritation, perhaps too mild to be even clearly recognized. Or it may also take the form of intense rage, accompanied by thoughts of violence, fantasied or apparently acted out. It does not matter. All of these reactions are the same. They obscure the truth, and this can never be a matter of degree. Either truth is apparent, or it is not. It cannot be partially recognized. Who is unaware of truth must look upon illusions.[14]

Coming back to Gary and me, we do our best just like everyone else. We are not perfect or we wouldn't appear to be here. When we are teaching the Course to the public, we also realize we are learning. We know there is really no one else "out there." In our experience, it can certainly feel like there are people there, but we do our best to practice what the Course says and use everything that feels like a challenge, to forgive. If just one person in the relationship is practicing forgiveness, it can still work. It might seem harder, but it doesn't have to be. As long as you are not moving into a place of unhealthy sacrifice at your own expense, then it's totally possible to have a loving and long-lasting relationship regardless if the other isn't even practicing the Course. In our case, we both do practice the Course, so it is something rewarding to have in common. If you are in a relationship where you are studying the Course, but your partner is not, it can still work. The whole point is that you can be at peace regardless of circumstances.

Everyone has preferences, so if you are honest with yourself about what is working or not working for you, then you can start the process of discussion or making changes, while doing it without guilt, blame or judgment. Having preferences is normal. Even Jesus didn't always agree with everyone. If everyone went along with what everyone else was doing all the time, there would be no progress with the Sonship. It's important to honor your path by being honest with your life and what truly inspires you. When you are in a state of inspiration, everyone around you benefits. The problem is that most of us fear the present, because the ego's use of the present is to drag the past into it.

> *The Holy Spirit would undo all of this now. Fear is not of the present, but only of the past and future, which do not exist. There is no fear in the present when each instant stands clear and separated from the past, without its shadow reaching out into the future. Each instant is a clean, untarnished birth, in which the Son of God emerges from the past into the present. And the present extends forever. It is so*

beautiful and so clean and free of guilt that nothing but happiness is there. No darkness is remembered, and immortality and joy are now.[15]

The Course is teaching us how to use the present to reclaim our true power, which would transform all our relationships, because we would no longer feel unfairly treated by others. When we recognize we are making people act out for us by our interpretations of what we see, then we can make helpful changes in how we respond to them. The world we see (including all people) represents the ideas and beliefs we are holding in our own minds. We see what we want to see based on our past experiences. When we start to accept this, we can have more experiences of the Holy Instant, where we shift from the ego's interpretation to the Holy Spirit's. The more moments we have of the Holy Instant, the attraction of the body ceases. We will be calmer and lighter in our attitude; less demanding of others. Even the body will cease to attract us in the same way that it used to. We will be pulled toward the call of joy, which is of the Holy Spirit.

If you are currently in a relationship that is painful, it is helpful to remember that the pain comes from thinking, then reacting with the ego, not from the person who appears to be causing you pain. It takes experience to accept this, and may appear to take many years before one can truly be free of the ego's grip. When you understand that you're contributing to your pain by how you are thinking, you don't have to feel bad about it, because you can change your mind. Also, the point is that pain comes from the belief in guilt, and guilt is an illusion. This guilt needs to be forgiven. If you're experiencing an issue with someone, it can be healed *now*, not in the past nor in the future. Healing is now, because the present is the only moment we have. We don't live in the past unless we choose to bring it into our present moment. We also don't live in the future, although the ego would have us believe that we do. True healing is always in the Holy Instant. Jesus is saying, especially when you have a challenge with someone, to have faith in your brothers during challenging times. What you're having faith in is their reality as a Son of God. When we see our brothers only as bodies, we're actually deceiving ourselves. Do we want to continue suffering and feel this pain of guilt or, instead, exercise the power of our decision-making mind to choose again? Of course, be mindful if there is abuse involved. The Holy Spirit isn't in the business of suffering. Take care of yourself and do what you feel is appropriate under those circumstances.

There is a part of us that still has a secret wish to be unfairly treated. Being unfairly treated to the ego means that it retains its innocence at the expense of another. The whole world bases its relationships with this underlying thought. It has become so normal that we have become dependent on other people to take our side, which is the ego's way of joining. The ego's way of joining is to see how many people we can get to agree with us. If they don't agree, we feel threatened or dislike those particular people. Can this be true love? It's no wonder that depression runs rampant across the globe. The thoughts we think with the ego are serving a purpose, and that purpose is to maintain the separation. In every moment, we are either imprisoning or freeing ourselves, according to which thought system we are adhering to.

In my own life, I've been practicing watching my quick reactions to what people do, even with Gary. If I find myself reacting with a twinge of annoyance, that is enough for me to pay attention to what interpretation I may have made about something. If I see what I want to see, then if I become annoyed, that means I wanted to see the guilt outside of me instead of in my own mind. This doesn't mean I wouldn't speak up if it were necessary. It just means that whatever I do or how I think from that point on can be done with peace instead of conflict. Once you catch yourself thinking with the ego (and you will know by how you feel), you can then stop yourself and practice thinking with the Holy Spirit. This will help you regain control over your thoughts, although it's not always easy. Allow yourself some compassion if it takes time.

We all carry deeply buried unconscious beliefs about ourselves. Until we question these beliefs and discover the deeper roots, they will have an influence over what we do and how we act. Eventually, there comes a point where it is recognized that the beliefs don't makes sense anymore, so we let them go. This happens when we really take the time to inquire deeper into the nature of these beliefs. Everyone will do this when they are ready. It's no fun to look at fear, but it is helpful to look at fear with the Holy Spirit or Jesus holding your hand. He says that when we invite Him to look with us, it is no idle thought. He is only a thought away, because He represents the right mind; the correction for our mistaken choice for the ego. You can learn to do this with any relationship that is challenging for you.

HOW TO USE MEMORY FOR
A DIFFERENT PURPOSE

Another idea the Course talks about is memory and how we can use it properly. It says memory is something that is perceived to be about the past. In other words, the ego uses memory for its own purposes, which is to keep us rooted in the past. However, memory is also a skill that we can learn in order to remember our reality *now*, in the present moment. This means we can use memory to connect with our true reality in God by joining with Him in true prayer, and practice listening to the Holy Spirit. In order to use memory for this purpose, it requires motivation to make the shift from being stuck in a past thought or idea, to the present moment, where there is no story attached. Identifying with the stories of life, whether ours or someone else's, keeps us trapped in judgment. The minute there is a story, there is a judgment. This doesn't mean we have to deny the story, but instead invest our faith in what is real. That is something that can be trusted, because true reality doesn't shift or change. When we become comfortable and non-judgmental in our inner world, we can observe the outer picture without judgment, guilt or fear. This takes honest self-investigation of our beliefs. It might take time to work through this process if there is deeply buried guilt in your mind. It's okay. The fact that you are taking steps to free yourself from being bound by the ego thought system is a beautiful sign that you feel you are worthy of such effort. Bravo!

The section in the Course I was referring to above is called *The Present Memory*.[16] More specifically, it says:

> *The limitations on remembering the world imposes on it are as vast as those you let the world impose on you. There is no link of memory to the past. If you would have it there, then there it is. But only your desire made the link, and only you have held it to a part of time where guilt appears to linger still.*[17]

> *When ancient memories of hate appear, remember that their cause is gone. And so you cannot understand what they are for. Let not the cause that you would give them now be what it was that made them what they were, or seemed to be. Be glad that it is gone, for this is what you would be pardoned from. And see, instead, the new effects of cause accepted **now**, with consequences **here**. They will surprise you with their loveliness. The ancient new ideas they bring will be the happy consequences of a Cause so ancient that It far exceeds the span of memory which your perception sees.*[18]

In relationships, we are attracted to the past hurts we feel others bestowed upon us. At some level, we want to keep the past in place so that we don't have to really look at why we are choosing to re-live it in the present. I realize how difficult it is to let go of what appears to be a past event that you feel harmed you in some way. Sometimes a traumatic "past life" event can remain in the unconscious mind, and can trigger an emotion to come to the surface, leaving you with no understanding of where the emotion came from. It requires some deep inner work to uncover the beliefs we may be holding about ourselves that are keeping us rooted in past hurts. Furthermore, what we think of as the past is really happening right now, since past, present, and future are all one. It's only the person's mind that is choosing to hold onto something that it defines as being from the past.

The power of the present memory is that once you understand that all your power is *now* (since the only time is *now)*, you can practice changing your mind about the cause in this moment. The cause of what we think of as our ancient hates, born of guilt, is gone. If the cause is gone, a question to ponder is why would we choose to keep re-living it? It must bring us something we want. The cause can be changed to mean that no effects can come from a cause that isn't real. Guilt, being the cause of all suffering, is a made up belief. It's forgiveness that undoes the guilt.

I've been a spiritual guidance counselor since 2009, and I realize that in some situations it's important for a person to uncover hurtful events that may be buried in one's unconscious mind. This can be helpful because by bringing past hurts to the surface, they can be looked at and then eventually let go and forgiven. There is no need to over-analyze the darkness, rather understand what purpose it is serving you now by holding onto it. Once you uncover the purpose, you can make another choice as to how you wish to move forward, with a new interpretation if you so choose. The Course says, *Can you find light by analyzing darkness, as the psychotherapist does, or like the theologian, by acknowledging darkness in yourself and looking for a distant light to remove it, while emphasizing the distance? Healing is not mysterious. Nothing will change unless it is understood, since light **is** understanding.*[19] This is saying that the light, which is truth and understanding, is not separate from us, and therefore there is no distance. It is in our minds, right here, right now. The light can dawn upon our minds at any time. Healing doesn't have to take time, although we usually believe that it does.

The following quote from the Course is relevant as to how we can use the power of the present to be relieved of the effects of time: *It has taken time to misguide you so completely, but it takes no time at all to be what you are. Begin to practice the Holy Spirit's use of time as a teaching aid to happiness and peace. Take this very instant, now, and think of it as all there is of time. Nothing can reach you here out of the past, and it is here that you are completely absolved, completely free and wholly without condemnation. From this holy instant wherein holiness was born again you will go forth in time without fear, and with no sense of change with time.*[20] This is so powerful! You might want to take a moment to marinate in this idea. Let it sink in. **The true present is a continuous stream of holy instants. You are always safe, supported and loved as if you were being lifted up and carried by the wings of an angel.**

I'll never forget a dream that I had many years ago. I was walking along a cliff side in a very mountainous area. As I continued to walk, looking at the views, a very majestic and androgynous type being came up to me and lifted me up, carrying me on its shoulders. This being represented a strong, warrior archetype; not war-like, but very strong and peaceful in Spirit. The being seemed to be symbolizing for me that I was completely taken care of and there was nothing to fear; that I was always being carried. Then, it flew with me over the edge of the cliff as we started descending deep down into what seemed like a well of knowledge. All around me were books as if it was a library of some sort. It reminded me of the Akashic Records. Perhaps I was given a peak into that realm.

As we neared the bottom of the well, I was shown a large globe with a map on it. The map was indicating to me all the lifetimes I've had in certain areas of the world where I showed great strength. This was very relevant to me at the time, since I had been going through a tough time. Being shown lifetimes where I was so strong reminded me that I can always draw upon that strength when needed. Finally,

I started to rise and fly back up the well/tunnel at a very fast speed. I heard a deep and powerful voice say to me, "Edgar Cayce knows about you. Bye for now." I'll never forget that inspiring and powerful dream. The voice, in my opinion, was the Voice for God, the Holy Spirit. It was the kind of voice that has an undeniable truth and power to it. As I write this, the feeling of inspiration is coming back to me, and I'm truly grateful for it.

Whenever you have moments of inspiration where you feel something beyond yourself is speaking to you, just bathe in gratitude. We all get reminders along our path of something beyond this world, and that our true identity is beyond what our body's eyes can see. Beings are around us all the time. It's just out of our awareness. Inspiration is a useful tool to use in any relationship you are having that is conflicted. When you do your best to stay in your center, regardless of what's happening, and allow inspiration to flow through you, it will guide you to your next steps. You can trust that. Inspiration is the very opposite of the ego, and the Course doesn't sugar-coat the ego. It says the ego doesn't love you. Before I became a student of the Course, I used to think, like many other New Age thought leaders, that the ego was your friend. I used to say, "Become friends with your ego!" This is not the Course's perspective. The Course says that the ego needs to be undone before we can accept our true reality as the Christ, God's one Son. Salvation means "undoing." When we undo the false self, then the *real* Self can emerge; not as a body, but as perfect Spirit, one with God. In the meantime, we will always be attracted to special relationships as long as we hold illusions about the body. The Course says:

> *You cannot love parts of reality and understand what love means. If you would love unlike to God, Who knows no special love, how can you understand it? To believe that **special** relationships, with **special** love, can offer you salvation is the belief that separation is salvation. For it is the complete equality of the Atonement in which salvation lies.*

How can you decide that special aspects of the Sonship can give you more than others? The past has taught you this. Yet the holy instant teaches you it is not so.[21]

The best we can do as people here in a world of time and space is to practice the idea that we can use our life experiences to increase our faith in God, Who truly does complete us. God's love is total. Since we are having a human experience, of course we will be attracted and attached to bodies for a while, and our love will be limited until the time comes when we start to realize that bodies don't make us happy and neither does limited love. In fact, it's completely the opposite. What truly makes us happy is when we are not dependent on anything outside us to feel safe, whole and complete. **Safety comes from within, from thinking as God thinks, which means we share His certainty of what we are.** I've experienced the power of this over the years, and have often said to myself, "I just want to be free." What I mean is that I want to be free of the ego's games and lies. I've had to step up my own practice of forgiveness and will continue doing so until true freedom is realized within me. Aren't we all worth the consistent effort? The Course says we don't believe we are. This can be used as a great motivator to choose again. For a deeper reflection on how to do that, please join me in the next chapter.

PAGE FOR PERSONAL NOTES

CHAPTER 3

ADVENTURES IN TRAVELING

*The past is gone; seek not to preserve it in the special relationship
that binds you to it, and would teach you salvation is past and so you
must return to the past to find salvation. There is no fantasy that
does not contain the dream of retribution for the past. Would you act
out the dream, or let it go?*[1]

If there is any good test to practicing true forgiveness, you can be
sure that extensive travel gives one plenty of opportunities! In
some partnerships, couples do practically everything together during
a 24-hour day period, especially if their partnership involves working
close together by sharing a business. I'll be discussing how to work
through challenges with this, but also how to see those challenges as
opportunities for growth.

Let's not forget that this book is a guidebook for experiencing true
intimacy with your partner, as well as living lovingly and peacefully
in *all* your relationships. As a reminder, although we are focusing on
romantic relationships in this book, even if you are not currently in a
romantic relationship, the general tools and ideas here can still be helpful and applied to any relationship.

One of the keys in maintaining a sense of intimacy, love, and respect for yourself and your partner is to mindfully communicate. Use whatever challenges may be right in front of your face on any given day for the Holy Spirit's purpose of love and forgiveness. Avoid the ego's purpose of making sin, guilt, and fear real in your mind. If you practice the tools and ideas given to you in this book, it will help to lead you towards undoing error in your mind rather than strengthening it. This will be a tremendous help in maintaining a sense of intimacy in your relationships, because you will be happier and enjoy them more.

Gary and I travel around the world each year presenting our workshops, and when we are not traveling, we work at home together. We do practically everything together and enjoy the work as well as spending time with one another. One of the things we love to do is meet other Course students around the world and hear their stories of how they got onto this path. Gary and I also make it a point to remember to have fun, whether it's on the road or at home, giving ourselves some extra time to play, sight-see, and experience the cultures of the places we are visiting. This gives us some breathing space and also reminds us not to take life too seriously. It's easy to overwork oneself, leaving no time for rest, which is also making everything real in the ego mind. So, we do our best to mix our work with relaxation time. The ego likes to operate on the principle of "all work and no play." This is its way of feeling worthy and useful. It's this kind of mentality that contributes to stress and disconnection in relationships. It's easy to become so identified with what you do in this life and with your career, that you forget who you really are.

By the way, being spiritual doesn't mean you have to give up anything, or the pleasures that life on earth can bring. The Course isn't about behavior, but a change of mind. It isn't asking us to deny our experiences in this world as bodies. In other words, you can be normal and live your normal life, but now you can do it with the Holy Spirit and experience the happy dream. For example, when Gary and I were enjoying Paris during one of our trips, it seemed to bring out the more adventurous parts of our personalities, and there was a feeling in the air that we could do anything. What some people may not know about me is that I have a side that is very adventurous and even daring. This side of me can be ignited by certain songs that play on the radio, or when I'm drumming on my Djembe drum (Gary seems to think I become possessed when I do this since I really get into it!). It can also happen if I am in a somewhat "moody" atmosphere such as in a lounge listening to passionate music. Having a glass of wine doesn't hurt either to bring out this side of my nature, but I'm a very light drinker, and only drink on occasion, rarely ever having more than one glass of wine. These days, I barely drink at all. This wasn't always the case. I had my drinking phase in my late teens and early 20's (a somewhat typical teen-age experience), going to lots of parties in high school and college. I had those days, but I am thankful it was a phase, and didn't last long. There were times during those days that I played into the whole "victim" game. I would say things like, "No one understands me," as I continued to drown in my ego.

THE UNDERLYING MEANING OF JEALOUSY

Back to Paris, one night Gary and I got tickets to see the show "Moulin Rouge." This was the real deal. It was a sexy show, and we enjoyed it very much. The music and dancing was wonderful. It was the passion of it all that excited me the most, as well as the performers' fearlessly "raw" performance. Most of the women were topless (since it was a topless, Vegas type show) and once in a while I would glance at Gary to see his reaction, and it was actually fun for me to see that he was enjoying it, because that brought out in me a wonderful, passionate feeling of being fully in the present. In that moment I was making a choice to use the situation to keep the passion alive. In my earlier years, I would have been insanely jealous to see Gary looking at other women. I am happy to say I have overcome the whole jealousy idea. Gary and I are secure enough in our relationship where we can allow each other to be who we are without a need to claim "ownership" over the other. We're "normal" people just like everyone else, but we do know how to forgive, which lessens the length of time we might feel conflict with each other. I bring up this story because Gary and I like to remember to have fun and keep things light. We don't have to take the dream so seriously. Remember to laugh and have a blast!

Lots of us use a situation where we see our partners looking at someone else as a threat to our existence. What if we could all use these situations for a different purpose? Perhaps instead of reacting with jealousy when our partners stare at another man or another woman, we could remember that it's not personal, and we don't have to make it real. Gawking or drooling over someone is different than just glancing and admiring beauty, which is completely normal. Furthermore, what should we expect of special relationships? That is their purpose, to make the body enticing, holy and real. As long as we can laugh at this and remember the truth, there is no real harm done. When we react to a person or situation with our egos, it makes this whole ego game of life real, which leads to upset feelings and resentment. It's not that we won't ever get upset or angry, but there is another way of looking at the upset from a place of cause and not effect.

There is something to be said, however, about being polite when you are with your partners, so respectfully glancing is pretty different than an outright, long and lingering lustful stare. This just comes down to awareness that there is nothing someone else has that we lack, but only our thinking makes it so. In my more insecure days, I would get jealous if any of my boyfriends were looking at other women. It would ruin my mood for the rest of the day or much longer. I realize that I got jealous because I didn't have much self-worth. I interpreted my boyfriend's roaming eyes as meaning that I wasn't good enough, when it really wasn't personal. When I look back at those times now, I realize that I was learning how to really love myself. Those situations were opportunities for me to learn that nothing and no one outside of me has the power to make me feel small or less than anyone else. It is a choice.

If you find yourself feeling jealous, just remind yourself that you have chosen to look at the person or the experience with the ego, whose goal is separation and differences. **Comparison is an ego device**. Remind yourself that thinking and believing that you are not enough is an attack on yourself and ultimately on God. If you are as God created you, which is whole, innocent, and perfect love, it is impossible for you to be anything else. Jealousy is just a reminder that there is still some unconscious guilt in the mind that needs to be forgiven, and you can do it. To experience yourself as guiltless is to experience yourself as not separate from anyone or anything, with the understanding that when there is nothing to defend, you are safe. When you are tempted to project jealousy onto your partner, you can remember this from the Course: ... *those who project are vigilant for their own safety. They are afraid that their projections will return and hurt them. Believing they have blotted their projections from their own minds, they also believe their projections are trying to creep back in. Since the projections have not left their minds (ideas leave not their source), they are forced to engage in constant activity in order not to recognize this.*[2] I will get more into this subject in a later chapter when we discuss loyalty and infidelity.

"MAGIC" PRINCIPLES

Back to Paris again, one of the more romantic nights in Paris included a trip to the top of the Eiffel Tower. The romantic part was at the top, not on the way up. I was hesitant at first because I am not a fan of heights, and it can provoke panic attacks for me. I understood that I needed to practice forgiveness to make this work; that along with a little magic (*one* glass of beer taken without guilt) ultimately did the trick.

Note: The Course uses the word "magic" to mean anytime we use outside/external agents to attempt to heal ourselves, such as medicine. In this case the *beer* was magic. To be honest, if I had a Xanax I would have taken it.

My mental process from the start of our trip up the Eiffel Tower went something like this: *I am not a body. I am free. For I am still as God created me.*[3] I went on to remind myself that I am not guilty, so I cannot suffer. There is no separation, only a belief in separation. I said to myself: "I forgive myself for buying into the belief in separation. There is no sin, guilt, and fear in reality, and I give it to the Holy Spirit for correction."

When we stepped out of the elevator I felt better because I didn't make myself guilty for feeling the initial fear, and didn't make it more real by denying myself whatever it was that could temporarily help me in this situation. That is the point. You practice forgiveness, and then do what is helpful at the same time. It's not about suffering or allowing yourself to suffer. So, a statement such as *The guiltless Mind cannot suffer*[4] can be a very helpful reminder that you are innocent. Sometimes, a sequence of right-minded thoughts is necessary, because it helps to get a momentum going in the mind that can lead to inspiration, as you remember the truth, thought by thought.

In times of fear, you can also remember that Jesus or the Holy Spirit is a thought in your Mind, and therefore has never left you. Whenever you feel pain or are suffering in any way, remember it's your thoughts that cause you to feel pain, and ask yourself if the thought is bringing you pain or joy. If it is pain, choose again what you wish your reality to be, a body or Spirit, and then allow yourself to remember the truth. In my situation at the Eiffel Tower, I was taking it thought by thought, using right-minded thoughts of forgiveness to help me experience a place inside where I felt more empowered and relaxed.

So, we were at the top of the beautiful Eiffel Tower, and Gary and I spent about twenty minutes up there looking around at all the different directions of the city. It was such a beautiful time of joining for us and so romantic. Even though I still had a twinge of fear from the height, I told myself that fear (albeit an illusion) is just another form of excitement. In the end, I did okay. Needless to say, our night in Paris turned out to be amazing, not only because I was with the man I loved, but I was given an opportunity to practice forgiveness. I know that when these situations arise, it only makes me stronger if I take advantage of them, using them for a higher purpose and learning my lessons. Also, remember that any form of "magic" used to help you heal without fear is perfectly okay. It's the purpose it is serving that matters.

During our travels, we've also experienced intense weather patterns. One time we were visiting the island of Oahu and there was a major tropical storm brewing. Gary and I were spending some time with the dolphins at the Kahala Hotel near Waikiki Beach. Even the dolphins seemed to sense a storm coming. They were being so playful with us, but their behavior also indicated they were aware of something coming. Gary and I thought we'd better head back to our place in Kailua before it got too intense. I've always loved the forces of nature and I'm okay with being right in the middle of a storm, unless it's advised to stay inside. This particular night we probably should have stayed inside, but we decided to go out to dinner on our way home from seeing the dolphins. I've never experienced so much thunder and lightning before. We had an amazing view of the storm from our table as severe thunder and lightning surrounded the restaurant. The roosters that often roam freely were wandering around wondering what to do. It was wild.

I always say that if I wasn't doing the kind of work I'm doing now, I'd be a meteorologist. I've always been fascinated by weather events. Gary and I share this interest, which is kind of cool. I could be in the middle of a blizzard and I would find it exciting. I think it has to do with the idea that we are not in control of things here in the world, only how we look at it. It reminds me that there is a "higher" power behind things with respect to the idea that we are not bound by the laws of the world. We operate under God's laws, which are sane.

Anyone that really knows me knows that I am a positive person, which is something that has helped me tremendously in my life. There is always, without exception, a positive way of looking at a situation or a person if you choose to view it that way. It is a choice. Just being positive doesn't undo the ego, but it's a step in the right direction.

An important thing to remember if you are in a relationship with someone where you spend twenty-four hours together (whether you are traveling together or at home), please consider taking time out for yourself so you can have private time to do whatever you'd like to do. I have worked as a spiritual counselor with many people on their relationships. One of the things that I have found that contributes to conflicts in relationships is that people don't give themselves enough time to have their own personal space. This might not be true or needed for everyone, but for some it is very helpful. Even though we love our partners and enjoy spending time with them, there is still part of the self that has a curriculum that is independent of our partners. There will always be things that you may wish to do that your partner is not interested in. That's perfectly okay! It's very rare to agree on absolutely everything all the time. One night your partner may want to have a night out on the town, but you just don't feel like it. Or, he or she might want to see a movie, and you might not be interested in the subject matter of that particular movie. One of you might want to hang out with someone that the other doesn't particularly have a rapport with. In this case, it's not about making a judgment against your partner, but you are just expressing your preference. This is what I mean by following your guidance and honoring yourself by making choices that are in alignment with your guidance from the Holy Spirit.

Living in the world is not about being perfect, and we just can't please everyone all the time, which includes our partners. That is not even our job. If we all exhibited perfect behavior here, we wouldn't have any need to be here. It is very easy to step into over-responsibility, where we feel that we are responsible for how others feel; that somehow we can control an outcome, or that we *should* control the outcome. No one under any circumstances is responsible for another's feelings, or how another person chooses to think about something. This idea is not cruel. What is cruel is trying to take away someone's power to choose for themselves by making decisions for them, and even expecting them to be a certain way. If you cannot respect someone's choice to choose wrongly, or with the ego, and you try to take that choice away from them, you are teaching them that they don't have a mind they can return to where they can choose the correction.

To repeat an important point, most people have good intentions, and they want to help. But the Course says, *Trust not your good intentions. They are not enough.*[5] In other words, think about what the motivation is behind your reason for wanting to help. Is it ego motivated? Is there something you are trying to get from that person that you feel you are lacking within? Even if you can't trust your good intentions, you can *… trust implicitly your willingness, whatever else may enter. Concentrate only on this, and be not disturbed that shadows surround it.*[6] In other words, we aren't perfect here, so you can allow the Holy Spirit to do Its work as you work on accepting yourself as God created you.

TRUE JOINING

Experiencing intimacy with your partner is less about bodies, and more about recognizing that you have shared interests. In other words, you are not different from them in any way that may tempt you to feel separate, unique, or special. You have shared interests because you both share the same mind that chooses between the Holy Spirit and the ego, with a decision- maker that chooses between the two. Bodies cannot truly join, because a body in and of itself does nothing. True joining takes place in the mind, when you are letting go of all judgment in that instant, and thinking about that person for who they really are, which is perfect Spirit. When you practice thinking about your partner with this kind of spiritual sight, it leads to an experience of feeling close and connected to your partner in a way that is spiritually fulfilling and sustaining.

There is no question that when bodies come together, it appears as though they are truly joining. Ultimately, it is what's in the mind that matters and whether you are thinking thoughts that elevate both you and your partner to a higher vibration of love. Please note that I am not saying that you can't have fun and play here in the illusion, and do things that add to the excitement of your relationship. I'm pointing out that when you start from the premise of connecting spiritually in your mind first, where true joining takes place, then whatever you do, physically, is just like adding icing to the already delicious cake! Eventually, you might even find that you aren't as attached to the pleasures of the body, or at the very least, it might become less important to you. There is no right or wrong when it comes to how you choose to be with your partner if you both agree with it.

What we really want is to feel connected to God, and we substitute all kinds of things to take God's place, and these are the "special" relationships we have with substances, sex, places, to name a few. From stories of those who have experienced revelation, nothing in the world could possibly compare to the experience of oneness with God. Physical sensations would pale in comparison to Revelation. Our connection to God is what we really want to experience, and it is that connection that we believe we've lost. This explains promiscuous behavior. In this case, there is a constant need to make oneself feel worthy, loved, whole, complete, and accepted, when in reality you are already all of those things, and certainly don't need to prove it. The guilt in the unconscious mind creeps up and would have you believe otherwise. The benefit of practicing forgiveness is that it undoes the guilt that drives the ego. The more you practice, the more the ego is undone, and the less you suffer.

As the mind becomes more peaceful, you might also experience a sudden shift of interests in the kinds of things you do, or what you eat or watch on television. The more I've been practicing forgiveness, the more I have noticed a shift in my overall state of mind, which is more peaceful. Being peaceful can lead to all kinds of benefits that reflect your decision in the mind to be well. The effects take different forms for people. For me, personally, I've noticed that my eating patterns have shifted a bit to reflect a more wholesome "plant-based" diet, although I'm not a complete vegetarian. I still love exciting movies and programs, but don't care as much for the horror genre. The point is that natural shifts occur as a result of changing your mind *about* the world, rather than seeking to change the world in some way. This is normal. Practice accepting that your partner might be going through these shifts, which might feel at times that you are losing them. What is happening is that they are not the same person as before and so it feels like a loss. You might have your own shifts taking place where this is occurring as well. Respecting each other's growth and changing interests will help you grow together into the holy relationship.

MY RELATIONSHIP WITH GARY

Gary and I have a lot of similar interests in addition to the Course, but we do recognize that we don't always share the same excitement about certain topics. That's perfectly normal and okay. I don't know anyone who has a relationship where both people are in agreement about everything all the time or have all the same hobbies. A holy relationship is not about behavior or that you have to agree with another person all the time. It has to do with your attitude and how you think about the other person. Are you identified with the ego in others or the Holy Spirit? What do you choose to see in them? That's what matters.

In my relationship with Gary, I *choose* to be with him because I enjoy our path together. This is different than choosing a partner for the ego's purpose. If something comes up that needs forgiveness, I practice it just as we teach it to others. Gary does, too. I wasn't always this confident in my relationships. With practice and experience, I got much better at forgiveness and accepting myself as worthy of love and being loved. Even with Gary, at the beginning of our relationship, I wasn't always great at communicating things to him that I felt needed to be addressed. I've never been comfortable with confrontation. He rarely confronted me either. As I mentioned, we are normal people like everyone else, and things aren't perfect all the time. Forgiveness has helped us a lot with moving past any obstacles to peace. We've always had a wonderful bond and a connection that goes back many lifetimes, even if they are illusory. We enjoy our work together and laugh a lot. The most meaningful moments to me are the seeming small things he does for me and also when he takes a moment to check in with me to see how I'm doing. I do this with him, too. Even if it's a good day, I might ask him, "How are you feeling today" or "What's on your mind?" It's good to check in with your partner, and have quality time together. One of our favorite things to do is spend time at the park near our home, where we are immersed in nature. We have a little picnic, rest, listen to the birds, watch the squirrels and other wildlife that might be nearby. It rejuvenates our Spirits, and lifts our mood, naturally. Luna, our beautiful cat, is also a great joy for us. She reminds us of our inno-cence, and she is also very entertaining, wise, and a great healer.

I look back at the earlier parts of my life and I can't believe that person was me. It's like I've lived many incarnations within this one incarnation. That's how I experience life these days. You might look back and not be able to relate to the way you used to be, because you've grown, shifted and changed. Gary and I both feel this way about our childhood and into our early adulthood. We say, "Who was that per-son?" It might as well be another person in another lifetime. We were both very shy and didn't like speaking in front of people. It didn't seem likely that we would end up being public people, sharing the Course

with the world, in front of large audiences. That's the work of the Holy
Spirit. The script is written and we are just doing our jobs.

In the earlier part of my relationship with Gary, he was speaking
a lot, doing over thirty trips a year. I went with him some of the time
and would quietly sit in the back and listen. I didn't care too much
about being noticed. I enjoyed my privacy. At the same time, I would
find myself being able to answer the questions of the audience during
the Q & A segment, which I did in my mind. I thought, "I could be up
there teaching the Course, too." The process of taking more of a public
role unfolded very gradually at a pace I could keep up with. Gary often
encouraged me to speak more. He likes to joke that I started off singing
once in a while, then moved up to speaking for a few minutes. Those
few minutes turned into 10-15 minutes, which turned into speaking
for part of the morning, and now...we have equal time. We do enjoy
teaching together and there is a flow that happens that is effortless on
our part. That is also the Holy Spirit extending through us. You will
always be able to tell if the Holy Spirit is taking over by the effortless-
ness in which things flow. This can happen in your relationships in general. When things are in their natural process of unfolding without it
being hard and heavy, it means you are following the correct teacher in
your mind. Relationships won't always be easy. They weren't designed
to be. We have to work on them.

Practicing the Course can lead to mastery, but no one becomes
a master without lots of practice and patience. Eventually, even the
need for patience disappears. Impatience implies uncertainty about
the future. It can always be traced back to the fear of death. This is why
we might find ourselves rushing around or trying to get things done in
a timely manner. We wouldn't feel the anxiety about moving quickly
unless there was an unconscious fear of death. The guilt in the mind
runs very deep, and this is why the ego needs to be undone. We can't
see the deeply buried guilt in the mind that runs the world. You don't
have to get in touch with the original source of guilt (the separation

from God). When you practice with the things that are right in front of your face on any given day, the Holy Spirit will heal the deeper guilt buried in the unconscious mind.

It can't be emphasized enough that we have to want the peace of God more than anything else in order to experience it. The ego is very quick to react to anything that comes along that threatens its existence. Jesus was a non-reactionary. He would have known that to feed the ego would be to reinforce guilt and separation. It's difficult not to react when you feel someone is mistreating you. In a case like this, you can assess the situation, and if it's a dangerous situation, seek help. You can always practice forgiveness later. If it's a more general case of a disagreement, but your life is not in danger, then you can start the steps of forgiveness more quickly, and bring your mind back to a place of peace.

I've always been fascinated by how connected we all are at the mind level. I've had some interesting psychic experiences in regards to minds being joined. One example of this occurred many years ago when Gary was out of town. I stayed home, because I had just signed up to take a course on Hypnosis. I went out one day to attend a class. During the class, the instructor started guiding us through a hypnosis exercise. Deep into the hypnosis process, I felt a startling sensation that jerked my mind to full awareness. My body twitched and I felt my heart racing very fast. It was quite scary at the time. I didn't know what was happening. I opened my eyes and the instructor was looking at me like, "What the heck is going on with you?" I motioned to her that I would need to keep my eyes open for the rest of the session. Later that day, I found out that Gary had fallen down an escalator at approximately the same time I had the strong feeling and sensation during the hypnosis session. Fortunately, Gary wasn't seriously injured, but did have some cuts and bruises from the fall. He was taken to the hospital and then discharged pretty quickly. I realized that since minds are joined, and that Gary and I were also very psychically connected,

I tapped into the energy and whatever Gary might have been feeling around the time of the fall. This just strengthened my conviction that we are not separate from each other. When our minds are in a relaxed state, whether it be through meditation or by some other means, we are more open and receptive to thought and energy. Even though energy is an illusion, in the dream it can be felt. Ego thoughts are also illusions, but it doesn't mean we won't have them.

I couldn't help but think that since our minds are so powerful, what if we directed our thoughts with more purpose and intent by choosing the Holy Spirit's thought system on a continuous basis? Imagine the power in that, and how much it could shift our experience of a person or event, and life in general. The quality of our lives and relationships would improve. After that experience of connecting with Gary, I respected the power of the mind even more.

Another way we can improve our relationships is to laugh more often at the silliness of the ego. The ego plays out in so many ways that it is worthy of laughter, not tears. So, to end this chapter, here is a joke for you: Once there was a guy named Bill who wanted a horse. On Craigslist, Bill saw a Christian horse so he went to check it out. When Bill got to the ranch, the horse's owner said "It's easy to ride him. Just say 'praise the Lord' to make him go, and 'amen' to make him stop." Bill got on the horse and said, "praise the Lord." The horse started to walk. "Praise the Lord, praise the Lord, praise the Lord" and the horse is running. Now Bill sees a cliff ahead and shouts, "AMEN!" The horse stops and Bill says: "Whew! Praise the lord!"

PAGE FOR PERSONAL NOTES

CHAPTER 4

THE TOOLS

The miracle substitutes for learning that might have taken thousands of years.[1]

How many times have you heard that being happy does not come from anything outside of you? It comes from within. Well, at your core you *are* happy, and you only need to awaken to that fact. Although happiness comes from within, it's not too often explained how we can remain in the loving center where joy resides. The key to happiness is forgiveness, which in part means that you recognize that you are not really here. You are still at home in God only dreaming a dream that you are here. The Course states that *An untrained mind can accomplish nothing.*[2] Another way of saying that could be "an unforgiving mind can accomplish nothing." Without forgiveness, there is no happiness. It is essential to train our minds to be, as the Course states, in *a state of miracle-readiness.*[3] This means that we have set an intention to apply forgiveness to everything that comes up throughout the day that disturbs our peace, no matter how big or small the issue may be. For example, stubbing your toe is just as important to forgive as getting hit by a car in oncoming traffic. It may sound insensitive to compare those two things as being equal, but it is all the same because both experiences are illusory or a projection coming from the mind. Any experience that is not of God cannot be real. This is pure non-dualism. Many people understand metaphysical concepts and can quote from many sources, which can look very impressive, but when those concepts are not applied to your life on a daily basis, it doesn't mean very much.

This chapter will focus on some actual tools and exercises that you can use to apply in your everyday life. Since Gary and I have chosen A Course in Miracles as our path, most of the exercises will stem from that thought system. Since the Course is a purely non-dualistic thought system, in order for it to work for you it cannot be compromised in any way. Jesus demonstrated pure non-dualism in his life. *Pure non-dualism recognizes the authority of God so completely that it relinquishes all psychological attachment to anything that is not God.*[4] We will all experience this state in Divine timing, and it is a worthy goal.

THE MIRACLE AND FORGIVENESS

I would also like to review what a miracle means according to the Course. A miracle is a shift in perception. It is shifting from the illusion of separation to accepting the Atonement for one self, which is the understanding that the separation from God has not really occurred. Being in a state of "miracle readiness" means that you are aware at all times of how you are perceiving yourself and others. When something comes up that disturbs your peace, you can catch it more quickly, and then practice forgiveness. The goal is to automatically forgive instead of automatically judge. This doesn't mean that you have to monitor every thought and action throughout the day. It means to be vigilant *only* for God.

The reason why forgiveness can be so difficult is that most of us are still forgiving through the lens of separation, which makes forgiveness something that is done between bodies. This still makes the world and bodies real. This is what the Course calls *Forgiveness-to-Destroy.*[5] Forgiveness is done at the level of the mind and has nothing to do with the body. This may save you a lot of time. Forgiveness is synonymous with joy. It is still an illusion, but it leads people away from error and not toward it. Being joyful is a state of mind. Whenever you are *not* joyful, you are not your Self. No one can decide for you that you are happy or sad. Happiness is a decision you make. You have a choice. That is why there is no such thing as a victim. We are only victims if we choose to perceive ourselves that way. Although it can certainly appear that there is a victim and victimizer in some situations, the key is to remember that we can only victimize ourselves by choosing with the ego part of the mind.

By practicing the kind of forgiveness the Course teaches, which recognizes the innocence in everyone, it will lead to true peace; a peaceful state of mind. An idea that might be helpful to you as you practice the Course's version of forgiveness is that your thoughts have not left your mind. So the world, which is also a thought, has not left the larger mind. There is no separation between cause and effect. If the world is in your mind, then you can change your mind about the world. You can perceive it with true perception instead of the ego's perception.

When you accept only innocence in another, and do not ask for payback of any kind, you are in the business of forgiveness for salvation, which is true forgiveness. It is time to take ourselves down from the cross, because each time we attack ourselves or another, whatever form it takes, we are nailing ourselves to the cross every single time, no exception. No matter who is the accuser or accused, this is still true. We are always the cause of our own pain. Pain is not something you have. It is something you *think* you have. In other words, pain is a mental process, not a physical one. When you are not forgiving or not in a state of joy, you are in mental pain. That mental pain can lead to the experience of physical pain because the mind needs to project that thought of pain outward so that it doesn't have to take responsibility for having been its cause. Pain and joy are mutually exclusive states of being, and only one is real. What brings us pain is thinking with the ego. We do need to be gentle and patient with ourselves when we experience any kind of pain, and seek for support and help whenever it is needed.

METHODS FOR HEALING

There are various tools and exercises that can help us heal. These involve things couples can do together as well as those that can be done on your own. The whole point of the following exercises is to encourage right-minded thinking that leads you back to the actual cause of the upset or pain, which always comes from a choice you made in your own mind. Forgiveness and meditation are tools, so I will start with reviewing the steps of forgiveness and then move into specific meditations that will support you in your practice.

Forgiveness, according to the purely non-dualistic thought system of the Course, requires some further metaphysical understanding, or else it will seem like your anger towards someone is justified. Our society often condemns people, placing them beyond forgiveness, where there are no second chances. When you understand that the whole world is a projection of the mind's belief in separation, which is a defense against the truth of our oneness, and that separation is itself an illusion, the following definition of forgiveness will make more sense: Forgiveness, then, is the recognition that what you thought someone has done to you has not really occurred because it is your projection. The separation from God hasn't really happened, because it is a *dream* of separation, which is why you are both innocent. As you learn to practice seeing another person as innocent in reality, this is how you will see yourself.

Part of forgiveness is also recognizing that you are responsible for the reason you are upset, no matter what the cause appears to be. In most relationships, we think our partners are the cause when we get upset. They may have said or did something that triggered an immediate, angry reaction from you. That reaction is a product of what was already in your mind. Your partner just acted as a trigger to bring it out. When there is unconscious guilt in the mind, anything can set it off. Having said that, you aren't responsible for other people's behavior. There are certainly consequences on the level of form (the world), but you are indeed responsible for how you choose to perceive it, which can shift your experience to one of peace or keep you feeling like a victim of circumstances.

When the Course says there is no such thing as a victim, please keep in mind that it doesn't mean you don't take action, if necessary, and take care of yourself, or report abuse. It only means that whatever you do, you do it with the Holy Spirit. You can let go of the world or people having any power over you, and therefore maintain your peace of mind. This might take time, and usually does. However, you will be doing yourself a favor in the long run, since you are helping yourself be free from the burden of guilt within.

STEPS OF FORGIVENESS

1. Identify the cause (of your upset)
2. Then let it (the cause) go
3. So it can be replaced[6]

This means that you recognize that the cause of your upset has nothing to do with anything outside of you. If it's outside of you, you remain a victim. If you recognize that what upsets you is your mind's choice for the ego's interpretation, you can remember that you are a mind that can choose which teacher you are listening to. Once you identify the cause, you can let go of your interpretation of the problem (coming from the ego's need to project) and start listening to the

Holy Spirit, who represents the answer to the problem. Then, practice letting go of any further judgments that may come up, and just review the steps above if they do. You can also let go of the outcome of your forgiveness, lessening your need to define what should happen after you forgive. If you find yourself doing this, it hasn't been truly forgiven. This often takes time, practice and patience, especially with things that seem very traumatizing, so please allow yourself time to heal.

Forgiveness is a process that occurs over time, in most cases. Sometimes it can take years. If you find that this is the case, you might try going back to the mind and identifying any judgments or beliefs you may be holding that are blocking you from fully letting it go. Even if you find it difficult to do that much, you can practice forgiving yourself for that as well. **The point is that your innocence remains intact regardless of what stage you are at in your forgiveness process.**

Since meditation is another powerful tool one can use to make the shift from conflict to peace, following are three actual examples of meditations that couples can do together. The following meditations can be found on the *Meditation for Couples* CD that Gary and I produced together, which is a guided meditation CD that includes music that I composed. The first example is a meditation for intimacy; the second is a meditation for self-forgiveness, and the third for resolving conflict in partnership. Each example starts with the same introduction for preparation of the actual meditation. **NOTE:** The content in these meditations can be applied to your everyday life whether you are in a romantic relationship or not.

MEDITATION FOR INTIMACY

Sit in a comfortable position; somewhere where you won't be disturbed for the duration of this meditation. Please turn off your cell phone to avoid any unnecessary distractions. Set an intention before you begin, allowing each person to state their intention out loud. Now that you have stated your intention, focus on your breath, breathing in slowly and deeply through your nose, breathing in as much air as possible through your diaphragm, feeling it expand until your lungs are completely filled with air. Then slowly exhale through the mouth until the air is completely out of your lungs. Do this now 3 times.

Visualize or imagine what it is about your partner that attracted you at the beginning of your relationship. There is a reason why you were drawn to your partner in the first place, so it is necessary to revisit that point of attraction to remind yourself of the first cause of your relationship where all judgment was suspended, and you were "seeing" your partner in truth. Revisit this time in your mind now. (pause) Feel that attraction deeply, moving through every part of you and expanding from within you. Feel the excitement, love and appreciation for your partner, moving deeper into gratitude for the opportunity to share yourself with your partner in this way, so openly and honestly. The more you focus on the positive aspects of your partner, the more you experience those aspects in your relationship.

Now imagine a beautiful ball of white light coming toward you. As it moves closer it expands until you are completely joined with the light. This light feels warm and enticing, full of life, with a pureness and wholeness that is beyond this world of time and space. As you join with the light, becoming one with it, imagine it extending to your partner until you are both immersed in this light, together as ONE, feeling beautiful, intimate, and exhilarated by being in the presence of one another in such beauty, strength, clarity, and love. Breathing in the light of your partner, feel the sense of deep connection you both share, both physically and emotionally. Allow yourself to notice and feel any bodily sensations that may come up along the way. Any sensations you feel will only put you deeper into the experience of oneness with your partner. Trust the flow of the experience, basking in the wonderful feeling of oneness and joining that is present *now*. Positively project this feeling into your earthly life with one another, knowing that everything you do with one another is for the highest good of all concerned. See and feel yourself enjoying the closeness you feel with each other, both physically and emotionally, while knowing that the greater joining in the mind is what facilitates the beauty of the experiences you both share on the earth plane. Take some time to feel the joining now, with no resistance or judgment to impose upon your precious time together. (pause) Thank your partner in your mind for sharing this time with you, knowing that each time you spend this precious time together, you expand your relationship to greater heights, to deeper intimacy, and to greater awareness of your connection to each other and to the Divine that is *you*. In love and light, the Holy Spirit leads the way, here and now, in all dimensions of time and space, then finally beyond, where all is *one*.

MEDITATION FOR SELF-FORGIVENESS

Note: Please repeat preparation in exercise 1.

Think of something that inspires a feeling of joy, peace, and love inside you. It could be a situation you've experienced, a person that you care about, a bond with an animal, uplifting music, or anything that helps you to feel the essence of pure love. (pause) Feel the innocence underlying these feelings of joy, love and peace. Allow your heart to awaken, opening freely and effortlessly, just as a flower blossoms into its wholeness. From this place of heart-centered loving, invite Spirit to guide you and your partner as you join together for healing in the spirit of forgiveness. Continue breathing slowly and deeply, trusting that Spirit is with you, and through Christ Vision, only sees your innocence. In the same Spirit of Christ Vision, see your partner's innocence, and feel their loving essence.

Now, think of a situation that involves your partner that seems to trigger mental and emotional pain for you. (pause) In your mind, identify any judgments you may be holding against yourself or your partner in this situation, remembering that the thoughts, feelings and behaviors you are experiencing do not define you or your partner. Please do this now. (pause) Continue to breathe, feeling each breath taking you deeper into the knowledge that you and your partner are completely innocent, free to love, and perfectly capable of Divine expression. Any sensations you feel will only allow you to go deeper into the process of rejoining with your Self through the will of God, which you share in equality. Continue to breathe deeply.

With compassion and heart, and joining now with your partner in your mind, forgive yourself for the judgments you were holding against yourself or your partner, knowing that as you see another, you see yourself. Say to yourself, *I am immortal Spirit. This body is just an image. It has nothing to do with what I am.*[7] As you think of your partner, say in your Mind, *You are Spirit, whole and innocent, all is forgiven and released.*[8] Feel the essence of the following words sink deep into your unconscious mind: I thank you God, for creating me to be exactly the same as you. In truth, I am as God created me. His Child can suffer nothing. And I am His Child. I recognize that any upset I feel is caused by my own thoughts, which are then projected outward. If I think my partner is guilty, and it is *my* projection, then the imagined guilt and fear is in *me*. Since the separation from God did not really occur, I forgive both of us for what hasn't really happened in reality. Now there is only innocence, and I join with the Holy Spirit in peace.

Continue to breathe deeply, feeling lighter, and so relaxed and at peace. Thank your partner in your mind for participating with you in this healing journey with Spirit. Give thanks to yourself for being kind to yourself by practicing forgiveness in service to your growth and well-being. Your partner is a gift to you, as you are to them. Every minute and every second gives you a chance to love. Bless these opportunities to recognize your innocence, and give thanks to God that only *love* is real.

MEDITATION FOR RESOLVING CONFLICT

Note: Please repeat preparation in exercise 1.

Invite the Holy Spirit to participate with you in managing the details of your particular conflict with your partner. All it takes is a little willingness on your part to do the work necessary to experience deep healing of any and all conflicts you may be currently experiencing. Silently, take a moment to acknowledge the particular event, person or situation that triggered the unresolved feelings inside of you. Identify the feelings you have associated with this situation such as hurt, anger, or fear. (pause) Breathing slowly and deeply, feel the presence of the Holy Spirit beside you as you move into acceptance of the situation and your partner, understanding that life is filled with the exact learning opportunities necessary to bring healing to any unresolved issues inside of you. No matter what you think, say, or do, you are still a perfect Child of God, Holy in His Sight, and forever innocent of any charges you may have placed against yourself. Your partner is the same perfect Child of God. As you heal the hurt feelings inside, you are free to be who you really are. Take one hundred percent responsibility for the feelings you choose to feel in this situation, knowing that people (including your partner) do not cause your feelings. Feel the freedom that comes from taking responsibility for your emotional reactions. Continue to breathe deeply. Visualize or imagine your partner coming nearer to you now. Feel the loving essence of your partner who is one with you. Place your hand over your heart and forgive yourself for any judgments that you were holding in your mind about yourself and your partner, recognizing that both you and your partner are innocent, loving beings that deserve to experience nothing less than love. Take a moment and do this now, silently. You may find yourself becoming inspired to take some kind of loving action regarding this situation. Listen to your guidance and what it is telling you about any creative solutions that start to surface in your awareness, knowing ultimately that there is really only one seeming problem and one solution.

The thought of separation was made real in your Mind, and the solution is to accept the Atonement for yourself for having chosen to be separate from your Source. In the days to come, you might experience insights on what to do on the level of form regarding what you perceive to be the problem. Take action only when you are inspired to do so, paying attention to that still, wise, voice within; the Voice of the Holy Spirit, which is also *your* voice in the highest part of yourself. Listen with awareness of what it might be communicating to you. Now, continue to breathe slowly and deeply. Feel a sense of gratitude and appreciation for yourself and your partner for participating together in such a healing and loving experience. Be grateful for the opportunity to learn from all the challenges in your relationship, recognizing the great potential for growth and understanding of one another. In your mind, thank your partner for participating with you in this very profound, healing experience. Give thanks and appreciation to yourself for nurturing the beautiful Spirit that is *you*; and let thanks be given to your Source, for holding you in loving oneness with all that is.

WORKBOOK LESSON 121: FORGIVENESS IS THE KEY TO HAPPINESS.

This lesson is very important in learning how to forgive, because it first describes what the unforgiving mind looks like. It doesn't paint a pretty picture of the ego, rather it sheds light on the viciousness of the guilt that fuels it. Then, the lesson takes you through the following beautiful exercise of truly joining with another, seeing your interests as the same; what true forgiveness means. Here is the exercise:

Begin the longer practice periods by thinking of someone you do not like, who seems to irritate you, or to cause regret in you if you should meet him; one you actively despise, or merely try to overlook. It does not matter what the form your anger takes. You probably have chosen him already. He will do.

Now close your eyes and see him in your mind, and look at him a while. Try to perceive some light in him somewhere; a little gleam which you had never noticed. Try to find some little spark of brightness shining through the ugly picture that you hold of him. Look at this picture till you see a light somewhere within it, and then try to let this light extend until it covers him, and makes the picture beautiful and good.

Look at this changed perception for a while, and turn your mind to one you call a friend. Try to transfer the light you learned to see around your former "enemy" to him. Perceive him now as more than friend to you, for in that light his holiness shows you your savior, saved and saving, healed and whole.

Then let him offer you the light you see in him, and let your "enemy" and friend unite in blessing you with what you gave. Now are you one with them, and they with you. Now have you been forgiven by yourself. Do not forget, throughout the day, the role forgiveness plays in bringing happiness to every unforgiving mind, with yours among them. Every hour tell yourself:

Forgiveness is the key to happiness. I will awaken from the dream that I am mortal, fallible and full of sin, and know I am the perfect Son of God.[9]

When this lesson is practiced with sincerity, it will be difficult to see the person whom you are forgiving the same way you perceived them before. **A key point to remember is that if someone is projecting** their unconscious guilt onto you, it means that person is in a state of fear and is calling for love; for help. For example, you might want to try imagining that person and yourself as innocent children, both in a state of fear, and in need of a teacher (the Holy Spirit) to assist you in perceiving the situation differently, as a call for love. You are both in the same boat, because you are just as fearful as the other person if your reaction is less than total, unconditional love.

BEING A NEUTRAL OBSERVER

When you are in the heat of an argument or feeling very upset, practice shifting your position from being at the effect of the issue to being a neutral observer, which is also allowing you to accept that the cause of your upset is coming from your own mind; it's a projection. No one can decide for you *how* you feel. You are in total control of how you interpret an event. Watch your reactions with Jesus or the Holy Spirit from *Above the Battleground*.[10] This exercise of watching yourself with Jesus will allow you to have more compassion for yourself and for your partner. You both want the same thing, even if it might not look that way. You both want the peace of God. Also, you both *are* the peace of God in reality. If you see your partner this way, you are reminding your mind of the truth. That is what is missing. What you think you want from your partner is not what it seems. The ego wants vengeance, to be right, and to take something from your partner that you think you lack. The Holy Spirit will show you that you are both right (maybe not in form, but in content) because you are both the Son of God and have temporarily lost your way. Even if you feel you are right on the level of the world, what truly matters is...what is for the highest good of all concerned? Would you rather be right or happy? We will be discussing that question in greater depth in a later chapter. For now, you can think of this exercise as a way for you to step back from identifying yourself as a body in a world that needs something from the outside to fulfill itself, and instead feel the power within you that comes from identifying with your true Self as God created you. This Self needs no one or nothing to complete itself. It recognizes that it is already whole and fulfilled, because it has received God's true gifts of peace, joy, unconditional love, and eternal life. **Your partner is as holy as you are, and if you see them as anything less deserving of that, then you have defined yourself as unworthy as well.**

The tools mentioned above are some examples of ways to change your mind about yourself and the way you respond to situations, circumstances, and events having to do with your partner. **Remember, the *content* of the ideas in this book can be applied to any conflicted relationship you are having, whether it be with a romantic partner, family member, friend, or co-worker. You can tweak them to make them relevant to anyone or anything as long as the core meaning of the ideas remains the same.** When you recognize, first, that you are holy, it will follow that you will see the holiness in others. This awareness will shift the purpose of your relationships to reflect what it means to be truly joined with another in peace.

Speaking of peace, I wrote an article for the *Miracle Network* on the topic of peace. I'm including it in this chapter as another tool to refer to when you feel you might need a booster on what it truly means to ignite the peace of God within you, which you can draw upon in any time, place, or circumstance in which you feel you've lost your way. I hope you find it truly helpful in all your relationships, since peace is what we truly want in our relationships with others, regardless of what it looks like on the surface. Having peaceful relationships is a result of making the transition to holy relationships. There is indeed a difference between how the world defines peace and true peace, which I will explain below. I will also describe how I practiced being peaceful in my own life under challenging circumstances.

TRANSITIONING FROM THE PEACE
OF THE WORLD TO THE PEACE OF GOD

During the many years I've been practicing A Course in Miracles, I've noticed significant "power points" as I call them, where we have the opportunity to recognize when we are out of balance so that we can get ourselves back into alignment with higher truths. These "power points" involve choosing the miracle, but can take the form of becoming aware in the moment of when we are experiencing a false sense of peace, albeit the world's definition, so we can make the shift to a kind of peace that has nothing to do with outside circumstances. In other words, the world or people do not decide for us how we feel; happy or sad, peaceful or in conflict. It's a choice. The choice for peace is easily made when we no longer see the value in believing we are unfairly treated or in identifying with the ego's thought system of sin, guilt, and fear. Instead, we choose to identify with the Holy Spirit's thought system of innocence, bringing us back to a place of unconditional love; the only thing that's real. This choosing is the miracle. Peace comes with understanding what we are choosing between, looking at what we are invested in, and remembering that only one thought system reflects reality; the thought system of the Holy Spirit. Then, we need to have the motivation to change our minds so that it reflects the idea that we really *mean* that we want the peace of God above all else.

The Course says, *The mind which means that all it wants is peace must join with other minds, for that is how peace is obtained. And when the wish for peace is genuine, the means for finding it is given, in a form each mind that seeks for it in honesty can understand.*[11] If the Law of One says that there is nothing outside of us, it would include all people. Thus, when we decide to join with other minds, we are really remembering our oneness and wholeness in God's love. No one is really separate from us. If we attempt to have peace for ourselves alone, the result will be the world's peace, which is a false, temporary solution for peace. It won't last. What truly brings the *experience* of peace is to teach it by living it. This is how you make it yours. We are all teaching all the time, but when we choose to teach peace, our motivation for teaching it awakens it in our minds.

Another benefit of this is that we learn what we teach. I always ask myself when I am with people, "What do I want to teach?" If I want to experience peace and love, I must teach it to learn that it is mine. An example of how I practice teaching peace is when someone seems to project their unconscious guilt onto me, instead of reacting with fear or the idea of being unfairly treated, I respond with non-judgment and love. This can take the form of my not saying anything in return, or if I do say something, it would be to encourage the idea that we are not separate from each other.

The following story is one I share quite often, and it's relevant to my point above about teaching peace: A while back, I received an email from someone who accused me of marrying my husband, Gary Renard, for his money. My first thought was, "What money?" I was amused, but not insulted. I asked the Holy Spirit to assist me with the most loving response, regardless of the form the response would take. The guidance given me was to email him back and tell him no harm has been done. I really meant this. I emailed him a very short email saying, "Hello and thank you for sharing this with me. I'm not fooled by you. No harm has been done. I don't see you as anything less than God. You are always a brother. Perhaps we will meet one day." I left it at that. I never heard from the person again.

When there is no reaction with anger to someone's projection and you don't take it personally, it can have no effect on you. This means you are teaching peace and learning it for yourself. It also means that there is nowhere for that projection to go, because it stays in the mind of the perceiver. *Ideas leave not their source.*[12] Responding to someone in this way makes a statement to the other person that they are innocent, and their offering had no effect or consequences. If there is no effect, there is no cause, and ultimately, no separation. When your mind is trained in this way, which takes lots of practice, you will automatically default to the Holy Spirit's interpretation instead of the egos. Your peace will not be disturbed, because your starting point was peace (from the beginning). This is not different from the idea in the Course that says, *Forgiveness through the Holy Spirit lies simply in looking beyond error from the beginning, and thus keeping it unreal for you. Do not let any belief in its realness enter your mind, or you will also believe that you must undo what you have made in order to be forgiven. What has no effect does not exist, and to the Holy Spirit the effects of error are nonexistent. By steadily and consistently cancelling out all its effects, everywhere and in all respects, He teaches that the ego does not exist and proves it.*[13]

The above statement can be applied to anyone and anything as we learn to transfer this understanding to include all people and situations. Peace must return to our minds when we think this way. In fact, peace has never left us, but we chose to leave peace. Just because we choose against peace doesn't mean it's not there. It's just out of our awareness. What teacher do we choose to be loyal to? This is the ultimate question we can ask ourselves when our peace is disturbed. In my experience of practicing choosing peace, I've come to the understanding that there is always a benefit, even if it doesn't seem like it in the moment. For example, sometimes it might seem like you are giving your power away or losing something by not defending yourself or attacking back when there is a perceived threat. What you are losing is the ego, and gaining trust in the Holy Spirit. In my experiences with this, I've learned that the ego offers nothing but pain and conflict and therefore it is valueless. The Holy Spirit is truly valuable, because It knows only the truth about you and throws out any case you may have built up against yourself. This doesn't mean that I would stand there and let someone walk all over me or abuse me in some way. It only means that I wouldn't respond with attack in my mind, even if it requires me to temporarily remove myself from a situation. Forgiveness is done at the level of the mind, and therefore does not require you to be physically present with someone as you are forgiving. **Peace is remembered in the mind that forgives.**

I've often noticed that if I am not peaceful, and if I look carefully at why that is, there is always a judgment underneath the surface. The judgment might be that I am valuing something outside of me more than what God Wills for me. This can take the form of body attachments or investing my faith in my own perceived interests. When I lost my voice for several months, I was tempted many times to fall into the trap of ego/body identification, instead of realizing I could have let go of the ego's interpretation instead (which wouldn't have been a real loss). The gain in this would be to allow the Holy Spirit to reinterpret for me how to use the body for Its purposes. This is what letting go of our own judgments can look like. Judging on our own is the cause of all loss of peace. I learned so many powerful lessons during this time of challenge. One of the most important lessons that I learned was that I didn't realize how attached to the body I was until something went wrong with it. This helped me, because it inspired me to go inward and recognize what is really valuable; the peace of God. It takes work, which is the *undoing* that the Course talks about. It says, *Salvation is undoing. If you choose to see the body, you behold a world of separation, unrelated things, and happenings that make no sense at all. This one appears and disappears in death; that one is doomed to suffering and loss. And no one is exactly as he was an instant previous, nor will he be the same as he is now an instant hence. Who could have trust where so much change is seen, for who is worthy if he be but dust? Salvation is undoing of all this. For constancy arises in the sight of those whose eyes salvation has released from looking at the cost of keeping guilt, because they chose to let it go instead.*[14]

In my experience with various body issues, I made a decision that I wouldn't let my body be the decision-maker for me. Anytime the body was my decision-maker, I lost my peace. So, I changed my mind and decided that in no circumstance would I let the body be in charge of how I feel. This brought me much peace, because it showed me that I could be at peace regardless of circumstances. Symbols cannot have the power to affect your peace unless you give it that power. In addition to practicing forgiveness, which cultivates peace, I didn't deny worldly things that could help me feel more comfortable, or things that contributed to my having a joyful experience. The Course is definitely not saying we should deny our experience in the world. It does say, however, that the peace of God *denies the ability of anything not of God to affect you. This is the proper use of denial.*[15]

In summary, every day is an opportunity to remember our *real* identity. It is practicing forgiveness in our everyday lives that leads to true peace, because it undoes the guilt in the mind that believes it is separate from God. I mentioned earlier that judgment is the cause of all loss of peace. The first judgment that was made was the Son's belief that God's home was now a place to be feared. Peace was forgotten as the guilt over this judgment took over. However, just because we forgot *the peace of God which passeth understanding*[16] doesn't mean the peace of God is obliterated from our minds. It means we will inevitably return to our natural, peaceful state because it never truly left us, as we never truly left God. (End of my article)

Our relationships can be used for the purpose of peace if we truly desire it. We've been trained to perceive relationships as the means for getting something. What if you could be with your partner and not need them to fulfill you? If you go into the relationship already feeling whole, there would be no need for anything. You'd be with that person, because you just enjoy sharing your life with them. The more the ego is undone, the less need there will be to project your unconscious guilt onto your partner, which means a more peaceful, love-filled relationship. Many people aren't comfortable being with themselves, because when it's quiet their thoughts become more apparent to them and they have to look at them. There is also no one there to project their thoughts onto. If they are filled with judgments and grievances, it will most likely be uncomfortable to be in a quiet space with themselves for a long period of time. Lots of people like to have noise around them all the time, or be out at a coffee shop doing their work surrounded by people. There is an underlying need for connection with others. For some, this is a genuine feeling of enjoying the busyness around them. For others, it may be a way of hiding from being with themselves, since it brings more thoughts to the surface. If this is the case, there is no need to feel guilty about it, but notice if being with yourself triggers a feeling of being alone. The idea is to remember that even if it seems like you are physically alone, it is a false experience. Spirit is all around you all the time, but it's out of your awareness. This is why finding time to connect with God through something like True Prayer can be really helpful to mitigate the feeling of being lonely.

The relationship you have with yourself is so important, because if you are at peace with yourself, there will be nothing to miss. If you don't value yourself, it can show up as feeling like something is amiss. *Whenever you question your value, say: God Himself is incomplete without me. Remember this when the ego speaks, and you will not hear it.*[17] This means the ego's voice will be replaced with God's love, and you will know your worth.

PAGE FOR PERSONAL NOTES

CHAPTER 5

PERCEPTION IS
INTERPRETATION

You should look out from the perception of your own holiness to the holiness of others.[1]

There was a comedy television show back in the late seventies/ early eighties called "Three's Company." It starred John Ritter as a young Chef, living with two women, played by Joyce DeWitt and Suzanne Somers. At that time, people were much more conservative about the idea of a man living with two women. John Ritter's character (Jack) had to pretend he was gay so that the landlord would allow the three of them to live together. As you can imagine, this produced some very funny scenes! Jack loved women, but he was also a really good guy. The funny aspect about the show was that there was always a misunderstanding between all the characters, because what their body's eyes were seeing or their ears were hearing was all based on their perceptions and interpretations. If they had really investigated what was really happening instead of basing their perceptions only on what their five senses were telling them, there wouldn't have been those misunderstandings. Since the show was a comedy, it did a great job bringing light and humor to all the ways in which one can misinterpret something, especially having a man living with two women. Near the end of every episode, the misunderstanding was brought to resolution as the characters learned that they had misjudged the situation.

Inaccurate interpretations happen every day, and they aren't always as funny as depicted in the show above. The Course talks about the idea that we see what we want to see. We will always default to the ego's interpretation until we realize that not everything is exactly as it seems on the surface. People do and say things for a variety of reasons that we can't understand unless we have the big picture. Searching for meaning behind what people say and do is a more helpful way to avoid misunderstandings that can lead to conflict.

HOW TO TELL IF YOU ARE LISTENING TO THE HOLY SPIRIT OR THE EGO

As a reminder, you can think of the ego as the thought of separation. In this sense, the word "separation" is synonymous with illusion. There is, however, a proper use of separation, which is to separate out the false from the true; the ego from the Holy Spirit. It would be very helpful to be able to discern which voice you are listening to, especially in challenging situations or when you are tempted to judge someone based only on what's on the surface. One of the most popular questions we receive at our workshops is: "How do I know whether I'm listening to the Holy Spirit or the ego?" When this question is answered, it will help you to shift the way you communicate with people in general, including your partner. I'm going to answer this question right now, but please keep in mind that you may not always be able to tell which voice you are listening to since the ego is very clever.

For starters, I often use the following ideas from the Course to help me determine which voice I am listening to in any given moment: Jesus says, *You have one test, as sure as God, by which to recognize if what you learned is true. If you are wholly free of fear of any kind, and if all those who meet or even think of you share in your perfect peace, then you can be sure that you have learned God's lesson, and not your own.*[2]

Here are additional ways to help you discern the difference between the two:

The information you receive will inspire peace within you.

It will feel like the message didn't come from you.

An idea might pop into your mind, and it will feel like there was no effort in thinking at all.

There will be no doubt, only certainty.

The message will be loving in nature, and free of judgment. Look for the quality of the message.

You will feel a sense of joy, calmness, and clarity.

Fear will be absent.

Note: One of the passages in the Course, which can help you to know whether it's the Holy Spirit's Voice talking, contains the following questions: *How do you feel? Is peace in your awareness? Are you certain which way you go? And are you sure the goal of Heaven can be reached?*[3] If you can answer these questions positively and with certainty, then you can be sure you are thinking with the Holy Spirit. If you cannot, a kind thing to do is gently forgive yourself and set your intention to find clarity, trusting you will be guided.

Now, to be able to tell if it's the ego's voice you are listening to, just reverse the above statements so it reads like this:

*The information you receive will **not** inspire peace within you. It will be motivated by fear.*

*It will feel like the message **did** come from you. (the ego)*

The idea will be forced in your mind, and it will feel like there is great effort involved.

There will be no certainty, only doubt.

The message will be fearful in nature, and full of judgment.

You will feel a sense of frustration, anxiety, and confusion.

Fear will be present.

Let this be a guide to help you decide for yourselves which teacher you are choosing in any given moment. To get the guidance you would like, just ask. Then, wait and listen. Once you are as certain as you can be that your guidance is coming from the Holy Spirit, the next step is to trust in what you've received and let it go, which is the hardest part. Catch yourself if you start to question it. The ego will always try to interfere, especially if it knows you are listening to the Holy Spirit. The ego's voice usually speaks first and is the loudest. It will tempt you to doubt what you are hearing. You can practice doing this exercise when you are in conflict with your partner or anyone you are having difficulty with.

What we are all learning is to trust in our inner resources. This is what we are learning when we attempt to meditate. We are learning that we can trust going within and that we will be safe in our minds. Remember, the ego is terrified of returning to the mind where it thinks it will be found guilty, and then punished by God Himself. Jesus says, *What if you looked within and saw no sin?*[4] In other words, we are truly sinless and exactly the same as God. This is blasphemy to the ego, because it wants us to believe we are sinful creatures, as its way of maintaining its existence and making the body real. To return to the mind and find we are innocent is death to the ego. This is our fear. **Remember…sin is impossible**.

How can this information be useful and applied to your relationships? For starters, when you are mindful about being in touch with the Holy Spirit throughout your days, it can save you countless arguments with your partner or with anyone. Why? The answer is that you are learning to respond and act from a place of love rather than fear. The first step is to pause before you act or respond. The ego is reactionary and likes to abruptly react, but when you are in your "right mind" there will be a pause, and you will think first about which place inside your response is coming from. This takes practice. You are exercising the muscle of your mind. If your partner (or anyone) asks something of you and you respond with quick opposition, it is the ego talking. Perhaps the other person thinks that their request to you is what will bring them salvation, but if you respond with quick opposition, you are also saying that *your* salvation lies in not answering their request. So, pause and think first before you react.

As a reminder, two questions that I like to ask myself when I'm not sure what to do in a situation or how to respond is: *What is the most loving thought I can hold right now? Or, what is the most loving thing I can do right now?* (if the situation calls for some action). When you ask these questions, ask them with the Holy Spirit. Asking these questions will inspire a response, and it will most likely be a loving response. Remember, perception is an interpretation of a person, thing, or event. When you are having a problem with someone, remember this passage from the Course that discusses the use of perception:

*We look inside first, decide the kind of world we want to see and then project that world outside, making it the truth **as we see it**. We make it true by our interpretations of what it is we are seeing. If we are using perception to justify our own mistakes—our anger, our impulses to* *attack, our lack of love in whatever form it may take—we will see a world of evil, destruction, malice, envy and despair. All this we must learn to forgive, not because we are being "good" and "charitable," but because what we are seeing is not true. We have distorted the world by our twisted defenses, and are therefore seeing what is not there. As we learn to recognize our perceptual errors, we also learn to look past them or "forgive." At the same time we are forgiving ourselves, looking past our distorted self-concepts to the Self That God created in us and as us.*[5]

This is a very important passage, because it explains what happens when we use perception for the ego's purpose. It goes on to explain that forgiveness is the correction of our perceptual errors. If you find yourself in a situation where you are already in the heat of an argument, because you have judged and attacked yourself already, it only means you forgot to tune in to the Holy Spirit before the interaction. When this happens, stop as soon as you become aware of it. Then, say as gently as you can to your partner that you need to step away for a minute to clear your mind. You don't have to tell your partner exactly what you are thinking. Just find a quiet space where you can be alone for a few minutes, or however long it takes for you to get centered again, and remember your goal. What is it that you want to come of this situation? If it's to get something from the other person or situation at the expense of the other, ask the question again until the answer is one that will be for the highest good of all concerned. Invite the Holy Spirit to be with you. This will help you to become calm again. Then, from this more centered and grounded place within you, you will be ready to approach your partner again, and will most likely accomplish a lot more. This is taking responsibility for your part in the interaction. Instead of moving into blame, which is what most people do, this helps you shift from being at the effect to being at cause, which is in your mind, and where the only answer can be found.

Another powerful section to review in the Course that is relevant to the subject of mindfulness throughout your days is *Rules for Decision*.[6] This section is so important that I've highlighted it in my other three books. I recommend it if you'd like further study on how to go about your day in peace. Since I've discussed it in my other books, I won't repeat it here. If you'd like, please make a note of it for review.

The Course says that we don't have to seek for love, because that is what we are. We do need to remove the blocks to the awareness of love's presence, or the barriers we built against it. So, a helpful exercise would be to seek for any blocks that are holding you apart from love. Practice searching for the thoughts and judgments swimming around in your mind that are blocking your *real* thoughts, which are those thoughts that are pure, the ones you think with God. Thinking with God merely means that you share His certainty of what you are. This is what *being vigilant only for God* means. When you see yourself as God created you, others will appear to you in the same beauty. This is what is meant in the Course when you read certain passages that say things like (and I paraphrase) "The world in all its beauty will shine brightly before your eyes" or "You will see only beauty before you." This isn't referring to physical beauty, but the content of love in your mind that extends to others is what is beautiful; knowing they are part of the same certainty of God's love.

Coming back to relationships, your partner is never the cause of your upset. The reason why they aren't the cause of your upset is because it is your projection/your dream. You are the writer, author, and director of your dream. When you dream in bed at night, and then awaken from that dream, do you ever blame the figures in your dream that you were dreaming? That would be silly because you know you dreamed the dream, and there would be no reason to blame people or events in your dream that you know were not real. The Course says, *All your time is spent in dreaming. Your sleeping and your waking dreams have different forms, and that is all. Their content is the same. They are your protest against reality, and your fixed and insane idea that you can change it.*[7] This means both our waking dreams (those that we have when we appear to be awake) and our night-time dreams (when we appear to be sleeping). All our dreaming is a projection of the *secret dream*[8] of sin, guilt, and fear in the mind. The secret dream comes first, and then it gets projected out and becomes the world's dream. This is why the world seems so real to us. All we see is the projected world, not knowing it's coming from the mind. However, your power still remains in the mind to choose *how* and with *whom* you are seeing it. Your interpretation of it will make it real or unreal according to which teacher in the mind you are being loyal to.

As long as we appear to be a separate entity, whether on this side or the other side of the veil, we are still dreaming. And ultimately, we are still reviewing everything in the mind. Also, if our waking dreams are not real, then they are no different than the dreams we have in bed at night. Those two dream states also share the same content. We can treat it the same. In other words, there is no one out there to blame in a dream, so what we are doing when we blame others is only blaming ourselves. For a brief refresher, there is only one ego (dreamer) that thinks it's here, and you're it because you are the dreamer of your dream. This is how we train the mind that there is only one of us; all of us as one mind dreaming a dream of separation. There was only one illusory thought of separation. And furthermore, the separation from God hasn't even happened in reality. There is only a *dream* of separation. This is what accepting the Atonement for oneself means.

Imagine taking all this information and applying it to your everyday life and relationships. This is real power, which is the freedom to choose what you think, how you feel, and whom you are thinking with, the ego or the Holy Spirit. You are no longer a victim anymore because, again, you are the dreamer of your dream. The Course says, *No one can waken from a dream the world is dreaming for him.*[9] This means that if you were indeed part of someone else's dream, you would not be able to waken from the dream if you believe you did not make it. You would be a victim of another's dream with no seeming way out. Fortunately, this is not true. We are indeed the dreamers of our own dreams, which means we have the power to change our minds about our dream.

When I first started on this path, and putting these ideas into practice, which was in 2005, I experienced results immediately, although I didn't know how much work was still ahead of me. Sometimes things had to be forgiven over time, which is usually the case, but the point is that it works when it is practiced and applied in your everyday life to anything that comes up that disturbs your peace. For me, what really helped was practicing not making a hierarchy out of problems and issues. I'm still not perfect at that, but it's definitely gotten easier over time. To repeat (because repetition is necessary) there is only one seeming problem, and that is that we believe we have separated ourselves from God. There is only one solution to every problem, and that is accepting the Atonement for oneself, which is recognizing that the separation from God did not occur. *You are at home in God, dreaming of exile but perfectly capable of awakening to reality.*[10]

THE HOLY SPIRIT'S PURPOSE OF RELATIONSHIPS VS. THE EGO'S STRATEGY

In order to gain an even deeper understanding of how your romantic relationship with someone can be experienced more intimately is to come back to the purpose of relationships. What are they for? This can be answered on two levels: the Metaphysical/Spiritual level, and at the level of the world/body/ego. The purpose of relationships on the spiritual level has more to do with the idea that one is learning to grow in their loving with one another and learn their lessons of forgiveness; learning to remember their innocence, rather than losing themselves in the ego. The Holy Spirit wants you to use your relationship for the purpose of spiritual growth, which is to forgive, and this includes any challenges that come with it. To repeat, **our lives here are the class-rooms we have chosen to learn our lessons of forgiveness.**

The ego's purpose of relationships on the other hand, is to use the people in your lives to project your unconscious guilt onto, so you can blame them for the cause of your upset, which maintains your innocence. The process of dissociation is taking something that you find unacceptable or disturbing within you, and then projecting it out, so the imagined sin, guilt, and fear is no longer in you, but in somebody else, something outside of you. This started with the belief that we separated from God, which caused us to feel guilty, then to fear God's punishment. So, the special relationships we have in the world are a projection of this "tiny, mad idea" that we spoke about earlier. That is the ego's purpose for relationships.

Once you begin to see clearly the distinction between the two purposes, you can start to bring healing to your relationships. If you are currently in a romantic relationship with someone, take a moment to think back to what it was at the beginning that attracted you to this person. This exercise is touched upon in our *Meditation for Couples* CD in the *Meditation for Intimacy*, which you read about in the last chapter. Usually, when two people meet and fall in love, it's all very exciting at the beginning. There are a couple of reasons for this: First, the couple hasn't been together long enough to project their unconscious guilt onto the other person. When people are together long enough, what happens is that unresolved material starts coming to the surface and it's usually triggered by the other person. It's not that the unresolved material wasn't there before; it indeed was there before. Now, because of the dynamic of projection, the disturbance is seen as something outside of oneself rather than within, which was where it was all along. The ego wants you to believe that it's the other person's fault. They are the cause of your upset. This way, you get to be the innocent victim, thus maintain the image of the separated self. So, at the beginning of a relationship, this whole dynamic hasn't taken place yet, since it takes a while for the guilt to play itself out, occurring over time.

Secondly, it is indeed true that people choose to see the best version of themselves at the beginning of a relationship. You are truly attracted to those qualities in others that show their light because that is what you want to see at the beginning, and that is also what the other person wants you to see. So, these wonderful, loving qualities last until something comes up that triggers an ego reaction, and the viciousness of the ego starts playing itself out.

This brings up an interesting point. You always see what you want to see, and experience what you want to experience. There are no exceptions to this. You might say, "Of course I don't want to experience having an argument with my partner. That would be silly." Well, no one consciously chooses this. We are actually driven by the guilt in the unconscious mind. So, the ego (unconsciously) wants you to have an argument and be upset, because again, it is its way of making the body real, and making the ideas of sin, guilt, and fear real in the mind. This is a trick of the ego, making you forget that you have a mind that you can return to where you can make a different choice as to how you think about things. The ego likes to keep this game going so it can remain the helpless victim. "It's not *my* fault!" it says. "It's *your* fault! *You* did this to *me*!" Let's remember the idea that unresolved issues were already in place before you met your partner. If this is true, and it is indeed true, then the only reason we judge or condemn another is because we first made those judgments real in our own minds then projected them out. The world and bodies are an effect, not the decision-makers.

When these lessons are learned, you will suffer less, or not at all. I cannot express enough the importance of practicing true forgiveness, which undoes the guilt in the mind that leads to destructive behavior. Although it's what's in the mind that is most important, destructive behavior is fueled by the guilt in the mind, so when you take care of the mind by nurturing it with forgiving thoughts, the body/level of form takes care of itself.

As you can probably imagine, the sense of freedom that comes from living at cause instead of effect, is priceless. You no longer have to play the role of victim, nor would you want to.

When you are not a victim, you are free.

When the world holds no more power to take away your peace, you are free.

When you recognize that the power is in your mind and not in the world, you are free.

When no one can hurt you anymore by their words, and even their actions, you are free.

When you finally forgive the entire world, you *awaken*.

I am reminded of another passage in the Course that is relevant in regards to how to think of others: *Show him that he cannot hurt you and hold nothing against him, or you hold it against yourself. This is the meaning of "turning the other cheek.*[11] In other words, you are making a statement of your wholeness, and teaching it to others so they can learn that they have the ability to choose it as well. There is no question that the body can be hurt, abused, tortured, and even killed (in the illusion). But no one or nothing can affect the peace of God in your mind unless you give it power to do so. In a related topic, we will discuss the idea of abundance being in the mind in a later chapter.

The ideas presented here are about taking all of the tools you have and applying them to any situation that disturbs your peace, no matter how big or small. It is in doing this that you are learning to generalize everything, not making a hierarchy out of problems nor making some appear greater than others. However, when the ego tempts you to make a problem bigger, practice forgiveness, and be gentle with yourself. Be kind to yourself and others. I have always been an advocate for kindness.

The world doesn't need your kindness, but *you* do. Inner peace with yourself and your relationships starts with cultivating a peaceful mind, and the world will follow. **The law of giving and receiving can take the form of *being* the love and peace you want to see in the world by seeing it in others, and therefore you will receive it for yourself.** As a result of practicing forgiveness, sometimes the people in your life will change to suit your preferences, and sometimes they won't. The point is that *you* are becoming more peaceful and changing your mind about the world, rather than trying to change a world that does not exist in reality. This does not mean you should be a doormat and not act or respond to things. It means you live your normal life, doing the normal things you would normally do, have your relationships, go to your jobs, etc., but now you are doing them with a different teacher in your mind, the Holy Spirit. The ego will no longer dictate what you do or have a hold over you. You now know the truth... and the truth will set you free.

Being aware of the perceptions you hold about yourself is also an important part of healing a relationship based on separation. For example, if you perceive yourself as lonely when your partner is not physically with you, there is an interpretation underlying that perception that says, "I am separate from God, and therefore I'm alone." The loneliness comes from the belief that in order to be whole, you need someone to be physically present. The root cause of the loneliness is your decision-making mind having chosen the ego's interpretation. If you choose the Holy Spirit in this example, you would trust that Spirit is always with you regardless of circumstances. Your partner, being one with you in God, is also with you. Therefore, you could never be alone. I bring up this example, because many people feel lonely without their partners. The reason could be one of you had to travel for work for a long period of time. Another reason may be you got a divorce and it wasn't mutual, or you found out your partner was having an affair. Perhaps your partner passed away and you felt left behind. Whatever the reason, the point is that the ego interprets everything through the lens of separation, which is the cause of all the grievances we may be holding onto. When you understand how the ego operates, it gives you leverage since you can change your mind to start thinking differently.

I understand how difficult it can be to feel a sense of separation from your partner, regardless of the reason. A helpful idea when this happens is to watch your mind-wandering. If you let the mind run wild it will usually default to the ego's version of the story. If you practice focusing on the idea that you are whole and complete, it will help to reinforce the strength of God within you. Practically speaking, it also helps to focus on something that brings you joy. It could be writing, listening to music, playing an instrument, walking in nature, playing with your animal companion, or whatever it is that assists you in maintaining a joyful state. In my experience, my mood completely shifts when I spend time in nature and with animals. It reminds me of oneness. Singing and dancing also uplift and inspire me. It's okay to use "permission slips" to help you move into an inspired state and listen to the Holy Spirit. Sometimes we need them.

The experiences we have are influenced by the interpretations we are making at any given moment. If I perceive myself as being lonely, it's because I made an interpretation that being physically alone means I am literally alone, and therefore I feel lonely. What this does is reinforce the idea that I am powerless. Instead, I can practice forgiveness. The Course says, *Forgiveness is the healing of the perception of separation.*[12] Using the example above, you could change your mind to think about it in the following way: "This is *my* dream and my partner is a figure in my dream as are all people. I love my partner, but I know that we are not separate, because we are both at home in God as one, it's just out of my awareness. No one is dreaming the dream *for* me. This is how I know I can use my mind to awaken from my dream."

I continue to be inspired by the wisdom in the Course. It answers everything until we don't have a need to question anymore.

When that happens, Knowledge is yours. The following passage from the Course speaks about this, which you might find helpful in understanding your relationships and the need to question everything:

All your difficulties stem from the fact that you do not recognize yourself, your brother or God. To recognize means to "know again," implying that you knew before. You can see in many ways because perception involves interpretation, and this means that it is not whole or consistent. The miracle, being a way of perceiving, is not knowledge. It is the right answer to a question, but you do not question when you know. Questioning illusions is the first step in undoing them. The miracle, or the right answer, corrects them. Since perceptions change, their dependence on time is obvious. How you perceive at any given time determines what you do, and actions must occur in time. Knowledge is timeless, because certainty is not questionable. You know when you have ceased to ask questions.

The questioning mind perceives itself in time, and therefore looks for future answers. The closed mind believes the future and the present will be the same. This establishes a seemingly stable state that is usually an attempt to counteract an underlying fear that the future will be worse than the present. This fear inhibits the tendency to question at all.

True vision is the natural perception of spiritual sight, but it is still a correction rather than a fact. Spiritual sight is symbolic, and therefore not a device for knowing. It is, however, a means of right perception, which brings it into the proper domain of the miracle. A "vision of God" would be a miracle rather than a revelation. The fact that perception is involved at all removes the experience from the realm of knowledge. That is why visions, however holy, do not last.[13]

Most special relationships involve asking a lot of questions, because we are uncertain about ourselves and others. Although it's normal to ask questions about various things, when we start interrogating our partners it's a sign that the ego has once again dominated our minds. A healthy approach to this would be to practice clear, non-judgmental communication so you can get all the facts correctly before you act. When the ego speaks first, all kinds of judgments will be made that leads one to a detour into fear and uncertainty. Understanding why and how we perceive things (as stated in the quote above) can really help in making the important shift from conflict to peace. A key point made here is that when we call our illusions (thinking with the ego) into question, it starts the process of undoing them. How we perceive also determines what we do. This is why it's so important to look at our thoughts with the Holy Spirit. It will assist you in becoming aware of the connection between your thoughts and how you are feeling. **Honest, self-investigation is important in understanding what beliefs you might be holding in your mind that keep you from sharing God's certainty of what you are.**

It's time for another joke so this doesn't get too serious:

Wife: "Do you want dinner?" Husband: "I don't know. What are my choices?" Wife: "Yes or no."

As I write in my other books, humor is absolutely necessary, because it reminds us to not take ourselves and our stories too seriously. However, it's important to pay attention when something seems out of balance or is dominating your life in an unhealthy way. Although the Course says that you are not the victim of the world you see, it is still helpful in some cases to look at the traumas of your life if you have experienced things that are keeping you rooted in the past. It doesn't mean you are a victim if you are allowing emotions to come up and are dealing with them appropriately. What keeps you in a victim mentality is attributing the cause of your upset or trauma to something outside of you. This doesn't mean you don't address it or do your best to communicate with those involved with the trauma, if needed. Blame, however, doesn't solve the deeper dilemma of guilt associated with the trauma. Guilt is healed by forgiveness.

Coming back to humor, it's definitely one of the most important ways to remind oneself that there is another way to look at things. When you are laughing, there is nothing opposite to that in the moment that can intrude upon the laughter. I've often used laughter on purpose during times of great stress, because it reminded me that I was dreaming a dream, and the events in the dream (including my body) weren't real. When you are really laughing, you can't experience fear at the same time. You can practice laughing with your partner, reminding each other to lighten up if things get too serious. This doesn't mean you are laughing at the other's expense or making fun of each other. Together, you can remember the idea in the Course that says, *Into eternity, where all is one, there crept a tiny, mad idea, at which the Son of God remembered not to laugh. In his forgetting did the thought become a serious idea, and possible of both accomplishment and real effects. Together, we can laugh them both away, and understand that time cannot intrude upon eternity.*[14]

Our perception of time is that it's a real and linear thing. The Course says the world was over long ago, which means time, and all that it held, is over. If you have a partner that is not a Course student, it's perfectly okay. The Course is a self-study Course and it's not necessary to have a partner to do it with. I understand those of you that say that you'd prefer to be in a relationship with someone who accepts the Course into their life. It's normal to feel that way. However, you may be learning some of your most important forgiveness lessons, because your partner is not doing the Course. This path isn't meant for everyone. If you do your best to live it each day, your relationship can improve because your perception is shifting. The other person might not change their behavior in a way that you would like, but if you are shifting your perception to the Holy Spirit's Vision, which is seeing with spiritual sight, you will find that you can accept your partner the way they are and be at peace.

In some cases, such as infidelity, it can seem much harder to forgive since the mind makes an *order of difficulty in miracles.*[15] This means the mind collectively decided that infidelity is a harder problem to overcome than other problems. Even though it is usually experienced as painful, it often involves a deep misunderstanding between partners where each one holds a perception based on lack. Interpretations have been made that might have nothing to do with the root cause of the issue. Once this is seen and communication restored, the relationship can still continue if both parties agree. Since this topic is one that many people have experience with, I will be addressing it in the next chapter.

PAGE FOR PERSONAL NOTES

CHAPTER 6

INFIDELITY

Temptation has one lesson it would teach, in all its forms, wherever it occurs. It would persuade the holy Son of God he is a body, born in what must die, unable to escape its frailty, and bound by what it orders him to feel.[1]

Experiencing a holy relationship starts with the kind of relationship you have with yourself, which is determined by how you perceive yourself. Are you identified with the body as your reality or Spirit? Are you being kind, loving, and forgiving with yourself? Are you aware of your thoughts, feelings and emotions as well as what gets triggered and when? An unquestioned mind can't accomplish very much, but a trained one can. This chapter is an attempt to help you come from a place of empowerment and inspiration when dealing with a challenging situation; infidelity being one example. Of course, what we call challenges are really opportunities for growth. This is not about belittling your feelings and whatever emotions you may be going through, rather training the mind to question more of the thoughts that are swimming around in the mind and making waves.

When one thinks of being faithful or loyal in a relationship, it usually means being the kind of person who is honest, trustworthy and consistent in their character; reliable, and dedicated to holding a particular agreement with another person. The meaning of loyalty from a spiritual perspective has more to do with being unconditionally loving, as lots of us have experienced with our animal companions. What happens in some cases is that we confuse loyalty with imprisonment, making demands of each other and trying to control everything our partner does. When our partner doesn't live up to our expectations, we might feel we don't love them anymore. That isn't real love, only a clever mask for love, or "special" love as we've already discussed.

Real love is not of this world and cannot be replicated, although the reflection of real love can certainly be played out here in beautiful ways. True forgiveness is this world's reflection of real love. **We can only offer love to another to the degree that we love ourselves**. If you are in a relationship with someone who is not very loving, who is disloyal, or even hateful or vicious at times, it can only be because they don't love themselves and are calling out for love. If *you* appear to be the vicious or hateful one, it's making the same statement. Although this isn't pleasant, perhaps it can be helpful in understanding why a person behaves this way.

Faith involves trust. It is an understanding that the truth of your reality in God has not changed regardless of the circumstances of your life or what you believe. Faith is supported by an underlying feeling that no matter what happens, you are loved and being taken care of forever. Your partner is not separate from you, so he or she is loved equally by God. Any challenge you may be facing is an opportunity for forgiveness, learning and growth. An attitude that goes along with this is that your security rests on not needing proof that only God is true. The question then becomes, where are you putting your faith? Are you putting your faith in an identity/body that is vulnerable to attack, or in God, Who is invulnerable, perfect and eternal?

It is common for most of us early on in our spiritual path to put our faith in our bodies being our identity. As we progress on our spiritual paths, we start to suspect that the body is not the whole of who we are. In relationships, many of us put our faith in our partner behaving a certain way. In general, we might even place limits on his or her behavior as if we know or understand what we perceive. Think of the last chapter: *Perception is interpretation.* We expect others to behave according to the rules we put in place and the well-intentioned goals we set up at the beginning. This is an attitude based on a limited perspective. In addition, in a world of special relationships, this is normal behavior. However, even if both people agree to certain rules and are totally committed to each other at the beginning, why is there often so much inconsistency in behavior? For starters, as long as we believe we are a body (a separated and special self), we will fall into temptation, which can take many different forms. The rules change. In other words, we will always make mistakes. That's what bodies do; taking direction from the mind that chooses the ego, until we change our minds to an attitude that reflects the Holy Spirit.

Note: As a reminder, the Course says that it is sometimes necessary to place a limit on one's behavior if it is harmful to you or others. In the point above, I am referring to the ego's need to control or possess another, without allowing the person to choose for themselves.

The Course's definition of temptation (as stated at the beginning of this chapter) is saying that most of us are living our lives according to what our bodies feel and tell us to do, which comes from the ego thought system. The ego's very existence depends on the mind believing this. The ego's purpose is to have us forget we have a mind that we can return to — a mind that can make a choice — a choice that is inspired by love, and not motivated by fear. Temptation, remember, is one form of fear.

Secondly, when we do something that goes against our agreements, we have momentarily forgotten these agreements. In fact, a part of us feels that our salvation lies in that action. If we don't get or have that "special" something, we won't be happy, and we lose. What we are actually doing at that juncture is creating an illusion of happiness, because real happiness has nothing to do with the world or satisfying the body's needs. Happiness is a state of mind, a choice. Before you do anything, it is wise to ask yourself if you are being motivated by the ego or inspired by the Holy Spirit. To re-emphasize a point, this is not about pretending that when someone does something seemingly outrageous, you don't care or fail to address it. Rather, this is more about understanding the deeper dynamics of what is going on so that you can make the best choice under the circumstances. If something bothers you, it is a red flag reminding you that you can always come back to forgiveness. That is what everything is for. You don't have to forgive the "good" things that happen, or look for opportunities to forgive if you have no distress. I get many questions about this. Forgiveness is only necessary when you have lost your peace. If things are going well in your life and relationships, celebrate and enjoy, but most importantly, feel gratitude. Gratitude is an extremely powerful state of mind that lifts you up when you feel down. Gratitude is really about connecting to love and recognizing your true abundance as God created you. It can also show up as your life just flowing without resistance, and symbols showing up to reflect your forgiving state of mind. This is the happy dream.

The Course talks about the *Characteristics of God's Teachers*,[2] which means the characteristics you embody when you become an advanced teacher of God. In light of our discussion on infidelity, let's consider how Jesus describes honesty, one of the advanced characteristics of a teacher of God: *Honesty does not apply only to what you say. The term actually means consistency. There is nothing you say that contradicts what you think or do; no thought opposes any other thought; no act belies your word; and no word lacks agreement with another. Such are the truly honest. At no level are they in conflict with themselves. Therefore it is impossible for them to be in conflict with anyone or anything.*[3]

As long as our minds are "split," meaning we are not wholly devoted to the Holy Spirit, there will be inconsistencies in our thoughts and behaviors. This is why no one is perfect here. You don't have to be perfect, but you can learn perfect forgiveness. Since most of us identify with the ego thought system, we are trained, collectively, to judge human behavior as if we understand why people do what they do. Most of us grew up this way, with the assumption that what our body's eyes are showing us represents the absolute truth. We forget that there is another context in which to view our experiences, and that is a spiritual context. From a spiritual perspective, there is always something to learn from an experience. Our most difficult challenges then become valuable forgiveness opportunities. **When a challenging situation arises, and you find your partner doing something that you find unacceptable and disrespectful, it can be very helpful to make it less about the behavior of your loved one, and more about getting clarity on what the internal motivation was in your partner to carry out the act.** What is the *meaning* underlying the act. More persistent and loving communication is called for. This can help both of you gain a deeper understanding, getting your thoughts back into alignment with your higher mind.

What you do comes from what you think, but you can't be aware of what you are doing unless you question what you are thinking; what thoughts are in your mind? First, attempt to understand what is going on in each other's minds, and get all the facts before you act. Sometimes we might be making assumptions about our partners without having had any communication with them. If your partner is not willing to discuss it with you, your job then becomes to do your best to stay in your right-mind, practicing forgiveness, and listening to guidance on whether or not there is any action you feel inspired to take, with the intention that it be for the highest good of all concerned. It doesn't mean you never take action. Taking action can inspire movement and progress toward a particular goal for both of you. An action you take that is inspired can allow your partner to have the option to choose what is really important in the relationship, even if the action brings up anger or other uncomfortable feelings. Sometimes, being put in that position is how special relationships can grow into holy ones. It often takes something to "shake up" the relationship for one or both people to see what really has value. It doesn't have to be this way, but it is often experienced this way before progress is made.

A DIFFERENT PERSPECTIVE ON INFIDELITY

One of the most common issues in relationships is the act of infidelity. In fact, this is such a recurring issue in relationships, it inspires the following question: What do we think we need that we don't already have? Jesus says we have been given everything, but most of us look outside to get the things we think we need, forgetting that what we are really looking for we already have within. So, what are we looking for that we feel we don't have? The answer is God's love.

Since infidelity is a sensitive subject for most couples who have been through this experience, please know that this chapter is about pondering another way to look at infidelity. Another way is from a place of empowerment. This means we can remain *above the battleground*[4] — essentially shifting from victimhood to empowerment. This usually doesn't occur right away. There are stages to go through. Each person needs to work through some very difficult feelings. It's okay to allow yourself this process. Eventually, with an open mind, brought about by forgiving initial outrage, you will realize that you can use the situation as an opportunity. You will recognize that there is another way to look at the situation, and something to learn from it, which I'll get to. When we look with the Holy Spirit, we are reminded of the true cause of our upset, that is, our interpretation with the ego as our teacher instead of the Holy Spirit. If you have ever felt hurt by a situation like this, please allow yourself time to stop and listen to another interpretation, which can mitigate the hurt feelings.

Let's first look at this issue at the unconscious level. If we are really looking, at the unconscious level, at what is going on when someone "cheats" on another, and looking within the Course's thought system, the first thing to remind ourselves of is that it's not personal. Perhaps infidelity has more to do with how the person who is doing the cheating perceives the situation from his or her ego. It almost always involves a feeling of lack within the self, which is an effect of guilt. When someone feels lack, one of the ways the ego feels full, whole, and complete, is to be with another body, which is a substitute for being full of God's love. Needing another body to fill the empty hole one feels inside only temporarily fulfills the lack, because the premise itself is an illusion; the idea that one isn't whole to begin with. The action of infidelity then becomes a call for love. You can be sure that guilt is just underneath the surface, even if it's unconscious.

The person who is cheated against, in most cases, automatically feels upset because trust has been broken, and the tremendous sense of hurt and emotional pain that accompanies such an experience ignites their own unconscious guilt which the situation triggered. Guilt can mask itself in many different ways, and can even be disguised as love. We say we love someone, yet often that love is based on conditions, which means it falls into the "special" love category, as most relationships do here in the world. If you are in a position where your partner has been unfaithful to you, honor your initial feelings and allow your process. Remember that the practice becomes not staying trapped as a prisoner of those feelings. However, in most cases, it is necessary that part of the healing includes your partner's decision to acknowledge and take responsibility for his or her actions, in order for the relationship to move forward in a healthy way.

When your partner does something hurtful, it doesn't mean you have to be a doormat and not address it. I understand that these situations can disrupt one's life, and even end a relationship. Yet, it need not play out that way, and that is why I am writing this chapter. What you can do, after you have worked through whatever feelings come up, is attempt to understand what the experience is there to teach you, instead of falling into the temptation to blame, judge, and threaten. These are all forms of attack, and are exactly how the ego wants you to respond. This doesn't excuse your partner's behavior. Instead, it frees you from the burden of being a victim. Your partner will surely have his or her own feelings to deal with as well, regardless of what it looks like. Also, perhaps your partner's behavior is teaching you how to stand up for yourself in a way that reminds you of who you are — that you are really an empowered spiritual being, even if you temporarily allowed yourself to become disempowered. This is also true for your partner. They have also allowed themselves to become disempowered, falling into the temptation of the ego, or they wouldn't have felt the need to be unfaithful in the first place. At the mind level, we are all either guilty or innocent, but can't be both. From a spiritual perspective, if I see someone as guilty and deserving of punishment, I am reinforcing that idea to be true for myself as well. Communicate with your partner what needs to be addressed to the best of your ability, trusting that the Holy Spirit is handling the larger plan of your life. In other words, the ego will always attempt to plan for its safety. When you have the Holy Spirit, you can allow *It* to be in charge of the greater plan.

We think what makes us happy is getting rid of all our negative feelings through projection, when all this does is to keep those negative feelings in place. Remember that whatever thoughts you are thinking about another goes right back to you. Also, lots of couples separate or get divorced before they've attempted to look at the situation honestly. We'll look more closely at some ideas having to do with how you know whether it's time to stay or leave a relationship at the end of this chapter. Remember, whether you stay or leave a relationship is a personal choice you can make with the Holy Spirit.

EXAMPLES OF HOW TO STAY EMPOWERED

In regards to infidelity, let's say a couple has taken the time to sit down and discuss the infidelity and both are coming from a truly honest place inside about what they are feeling. In this case, the couple may decide that their relationship as a whole has a lot of potential. They are willing to gain a deeper understanding of each other. They might decide to work it out and stay together. Another scenario may be that either one or both decide that they've learned all they can from the relationship and are ready to move on. Or, perhaps the function the relationship served at the beginning is no longer relevant to one or both persons. If it's not a mutual decision, it is often experienced as a painful transition. Please allow yourself the dignity and respect to work your process. Needless to say, it is a forgiveness opportunity, and may need to be forgiven over time.

If there are children involved, it can be even more challenging, but still remains a powerful lesson in forgiveness. Open, honest, and clear communication with your children is advisable under these conditions. Children pick up on the energy and will do much better if they are allowed to discuss their feelings as well. Include them when you feel it is an appropriate time to do so, and if they are old enough to integrate what is being shared. Details don't need to be discussed if the child is too young to understand certain ideas. The unconditional love and support you give them will benefit them far more than specific words you say.

In times of great challenge, I prefer to remember that I am projecting this dream, and therefore I can decide to see it right-mindedly, choosing the love of the Holy Spirit in my mind. I then trust I will be guided as to what to do, if anything. Trusting doesn't come all at once, but it will come with forgiveness. To come to a place where you are automatically forgiving in your mind takes lots of practice. This is why it is important to practice forgiveness with the seemingly "smaller" things in life as well as the "bigger" things; it gets your mind into the habit of forgiving, so that when things feel bigger or harder to you, you will be able to forgive more quickly. **Having a challenge is a good time to reflect on what is most important to you — is it the world's peace or the peace of God?** For a review of how to make the transition from the world's peace to the peace of God, please refer to the article I wrote on peace in Chapter 4.

Inconsistent behavior in relationships can also trigger us because we tend to assign roles to each other, thinking that somehow we know and understand the nature of the mind and how it works. Let's take a look at Jesus's take on anger:

> *When you are angry, is it not because someone has failed to fill the function you allotted him? And does not this become the "reason" your attack is justified? The dreams you think you like are those in which the functions you have given have been filled; the needs which you ascribe to you are met.*[4]

> *What is your brother for? You do not know, because your function is obscure to you. Do not ascribe a role to him that you imagine would bring happiness to you. And do not try to hurt him when he fails to take the part that you assigned to him, in what you dream your life was meant to be.*[5]

We may not be responsible for another's behavior, but our responsibility lies in how we choose to respond in our minds. Do we add to negativity, or do we choose another response, coming from love. With an act of infidelity, sometimes there are consequences one has to deal with as a result. It can be a valuable thing to experience the consequences of our actions. Perhaps it will help awaken us to a new perspective. Or, in some cases it might even change our behavior to reflect spiritual growth.

Although the Course doesn't address specific behavior, since it's about shifting our perceptions, studying it for many years gave me a surprising perspective on how to choose to look at infidelity. It is this: Perhaps infidelity triggers us so much because, unconsciously, it reminds us that we (as God's one Son) *believe* we have cheated against God by separating ourselves from Him. As a result, we had a love affair with the ego, putting all our faith and trust in the ego instead of God, whose love is constant. The underlying unconscious guilt is painful, because we feel that we can't even trust ourselves to be faithful to God, therefore projecting our own fear and insecurities onto each other. Our guilt then plays itself out in many forms, and one of the forms, unfortunately, is our unfaithfulness to our partners. After all, if we can't be faithful and trusting in God, Who has given us everything, then we will try to seek out those "special" people or things in the world where we believe our salvation lies.

All of this isn't to say that you should tolerate behavior that is hurtful or allow yourself to be in a situation that is abusive in any way. It is important, however, to recognize how you are holding the space for yourself as you go through any issue. My teachers from my Spiritual Psychology courses at USM (The University of Santa Monica) would often say "How you relate to the issue *is* the issue." I always liked that statement. Also, there is no issue unless it disturbs your peace. If we go to the root cause of any issue, it is the belief in guilt. Guilt says we have separated from God and don't feel worthy to be His Son. The guilt over this belief plays itself out in various forms through the dynamic of projection, making it seem like there is a hierarchy of illusions or problems. This is the ego's way of keeping its innocence at the expense of others.

It can't be stressed enough that it is the ego thought system that is painful, and it makes the whole game of time and space real. We choose to live our lives in degrees, thinking some things are more serious or painful than others, when it is really all the same, because it is all equally unreal as long as it is not of God. Anything that can shift or change is not eternal, and therefore is not real. What *is* real is God, and God is perfect love. No matter what the challenge, it is helpful to remember what pure non-dualism means: *It makes a fundamental distinction between the real and the unreal; between knowledge and perception. Knowledge is truth, under one law, the law of love or God. Truth is unalterable, eternal and unambiguous. It can be unrecognized, but it cannot be changed. It applies to everything that God created, and only what He created is real. It is beyond learning because it is beyond time and process. It has no opposite; no beginning and no end. It merely is.*[6]

BEING MINDFUL OF YOUR THOUGHTS

Until we come to the awareness that God is love, and that we share God's Will, there will be hurtful feelings. Using infidelity as an example again, underneath all the hurtful feelings when one finds out the other person is cheating in the relationship, are thoughts such as: Doesn't my partner find me attractive? Why did this happen? What is wrong with me? Did I do something wrong? Am I worthy to be loved? So much of this self-doubt comes to the surface, just as the ego programmed it. After you've had a chance to process the situation, a loving exercise that you can practice (along with forgiveness) would be to start questioning your thoughts and reactions. You might want to ask yourself the following questions: "What is the purpose of this? Why did it trigger me? What thoughts am I choosing in my mind about myself that causes me so much discomfort or pain? Am I honoring myself? In what way may I have been unfaithful in my life? Am I willing to see this differently? The reason these questions can be helpful is that it reminds you that it's *your* dream and there isn't anybody else out there; not really. No one else is dreaming the dream for you. If that is the case, what is it your soul wants to learn?

You may be tempted to react quickly with the statement: "I can't trust my partner anymore!" In this case, when you are ready, an example of a right-minded replacement for this thought would be: *"What I trust is my reality and identity as a Son of God, and my potential to see this situation with peace. I place the Holy Spirit in charge of all my thoughts and actions."* This doesn't mean you deny your feelings and pretend that all is well, when you are feeling it is not. It certainly is important to look at your thoughts and observe them, as well as communicate with your partner, and even encourage him or her to look within his or her self. Then practice the best you can without judgment. This means you can look at your thoughts with the Holy Spirit, who will teach you to perceive everything with true Vision. Even when you do that, your guidance might be that it's time to end the relationship. The key is that whatever you decide with the Holy Spirit, it will be done without guilt.

Sometimes, depending on the situation and people involved, infidelity is cause for either divorce or separation from each other for a while. Perhaps it is a wake-up call for all involved to be more aware of what is going on inside them. What I am presenting here is another way to look at this from a place of empowerment. Most of us would likely feel victimized, at least at first. It would be very loving to practice forgiveness, and then do whatever your higher guidance is in this situation. It might be to stay together, or it might be to part ways, but please think about this: The situation might be the catalyst to wake you up to a more spiritual state of mind, to spiritual partnership, to inspiring you to question your life story in deeper ways you haven't thought of. From this expanded view, it becomes a blessing that everyone can benefit and learn from.

HOW TO KNOW IF YOU SHOULD
STAY IN A RELATIONSHIP OR LEAVE

How do you know if you should stay in a relationship? Ultimately, the decision is between you and the Holy Spirit. No one can decide for you. However, there are some guidelines that can help you decide what is best for the highest good of everyone. Let's take the example of infidelity, once again, although this can apply to any ongoing issue you might be having. If you are truly in love with your partner, then it will be harder to break off the relationship, even if "cheating" occurred. What is happening is that at a higher level, there is something important here for you to experience with this person — that is, lessons your soul wants to learn. It probably wouldn't be wise to leave a relationship as long as you feel there is still some unresolved material coming up. Also, if you don't resolve it now, you may later regret it. The same problems, if not dealt with now, often appear in future relationships until the lessons are learned.

Also, consider whether you are starting to take on your partner's problems and make them your own. This is not helpful to either one of you in the relationship. This may be a lesson you are learning with your partner in order to concentrate on your own forgiveness lessons, rather than the other person's. Another thing to keep in mind when you are trying to decide if you want to stay in the relationship is the question of your role in that partnership. What is the purpose of your relationship with this person? When you go high enough into a spiritual context, is there a higher purpose you can identify where you feel it is important that you stay together, at least for now? Are you having fun more often than not, and do you truly enjoy being with your partner? If the answer is yes, you may want to stay in the relationship, at least until you feel you've brought some resolution to it. This way, if you do eventually part ways, you won't have to carry into another relationship the burden of unresolved material in your mind.

Honoring your choices is very important, too. If you find that what you and your partner share is not something you truly feel you can build upon anymore, and it is not essential for your life, you can leave with grace knowing you've honored it completely. **Whatever you do, you can do it without guilt, so do your best not to make yourself or the other person guilty.** I realize this is not always easy, but with practice and determination to see things with the Holy Spirit as your teacher instead of the ego, it does become easier as you go along.

A common mistake people make when something very disturbing happens in the relationship is they leave the relationship before they've even had the chance to understand what it was there to teach them. I'm not talking about severe abuse. In that case, it would be perfectly appropriate to remove yourself from the situation and leave the relationship, especially if it's hurting you or putting you in danger. If it's a situation where you don't feel like it's a reason for ending the relationship, then ask yourself what purpose it might be serving? There's more to it than just what is on the surface. Once you feel you've truly understood the lesson, you can grow with the relationship in peace.

The following passages from the Course can be very helpful in returning your mind to the Holy Spirit's perception in challenging situations:

You respond to what you perceive, and as you perceive so shall you behave. The Golden Rule asks you to do unto others as you would have them do unto you. This means that the perception of both must be accurate. The Golden Rule is the rule for appropriate behavior. You cannot behave appropriately unless you perceive correctly. Since you and your neighbor are equal members of one family, as you perceive both so you will do to both. You should look out from the perception of your own holiness to the holiness of others.[7]

Have you really considered how many opportunities you have had to gladden yourself, and how many of them you have refused? There is no limit to the power of a Son of God, but he can limit the expression of his power as much as he chooses. Your mind and mine can unite in shining your ego away, releasing the strength of God into everything you think and do. Do not settle for anything less than this, and refuse to accept anything but this as your goal. Watch your mind carefully *for any beliefs that hinder its accomplishment, and step away from them. Judge how well you have done this by your own feelings, for this is the one right use of judgment. Judgment, like any other defense, can be used to attack or protect; to hurt or to heal. The ego **should** be brought to judgment and found wanting there. Without your own allegiance, protection and love, the ego cannot exist. Let it be judged truly and you must withdraw allegiance, protection and love from it.*[8]

Jesus is clearly stating that we have the power to withdraw our belief in the ego, even for a moment, since the mind that chooses the ego is also capable of choosing the Holy Spirit. He also addresses the importance of using your feelings to identify any false beliefs about yourself, and highlighting the power you have to choose. The Course doesn't talk that much about feelings, but when it does it is within the context of using them to allow you to see which teacher you are following in your mind. This is why feelings can be so helpful. Since there are only two emotions, love and fear, any feeling that is negative comes from the emotion of fear. There are many feelings under the category of fear, but love has no degrees. Love is pure and is always itself regardless of our many attempts to intrude our own ideas upon it.

I realize that most of us are not at the level of advancement that Jesus was in his final lifetime. This is why we need to be patient and understanding with ourselves, even if the ego wants to yell and scream at our partners and call them names. If this happens, it is still helpful and important to remember the law of the mind: Anything you think or say about another person comes right back to you. The unconscious mind knows everything, which means it knows there is only one of us. There aren't really 8 billion people "out there." When this idea is known and accepted, it can transform your life in powerful ways. You would understand that if you try to hurt another person, you are really hurting yourself. Then, the question becomes, "Why do I want to condemn myself?"

It is not easily accepted that the ego wants you to hold on to pain. On the surface, it's not something most of us would choose. It's the unconscious part of the mind that runs the show. Even though you can't always see what's in the unconscious mind, you can make tremendous progress by forgiving what's right in front of your face, meaning those people or situations that trigger you. If you are feeling peaceful and there is nothing to forgive, you don't have to go looking for situations to forgive. It's also important to remember that forgiveness is really the idea that nothing happened to intrude upon your reality in God. Forgiveness doesn't see "sin" and make it real, then attempt to forgive it. Instead, it acknowledges that "sin" is not real in you or the other person, and so you are both released together. Sin is nothing more than the belief in separation. Notice how opposite this definition is compared to the Bible. The Bible wasn't written by those who were close to Jesus, and therefore it is bound to have distortions. Passages in the Bible that speak of a loving God would be accurate, but not a God that punishes, judges or condemns His Son.

In closing, we are all experiencing ourselves here in a world of time and space to use time for the Holy Spirit's purpose; to extend love, seeing our interests as not separate from another's, and to practice forgiveness, which awakens us from the dream of separation. Let the world be the world, but you don't have to make the world your reality. You can walk the world, but not be *of* it. This way you can be truly helpful, and an inspiration for everyone who takes the journey with you on the path home to God.

PAGE FOR PERSONAL NOTES

CHAPTER 7

ABUNDANCE IS A STATE OF MIND

From your grandeur you can only bless, because your grandeur is your abundance.[1]

I remember the days when I only felt abundant if I had a lot of money. I wasn't thinking that abundance was a state of mind. Although true abundance has more to do with sharing the Holy Spirit's perception, it can show up in the world as symbols, reflecting your abundant state of mind. When we are having the experience of being in a body, the temptation to perceive abundance as an accumulation of material goods is inevitable. At some point, we realize that no matter how much we have, we want more. This is because we are using illusions to feel whole, but since illusions aren't real, the feeling of wholeness doesn't last. I realized this when I would go out and buy clothes or other material things that I didn't need. It would give me a sense of fulfillment at first. Then, a couple of days later, a feeling of lack would come up, so I would seek out more things to buy. It was an endless cycle until I changed my mind about its purpose. I realized what the ego was doing, and started joining with God in True Prayer more frequently. This gave me a much greater sense of lasting fulfillment, because joining with God reminds you of the eternal nature of life instead of reinforcing the ego's temporary gratification.

This doesn't mean you can't go out and enjoy shopping or have things that are nice. It only becomes a problem if you notice that you never seem to have enough. This feeling is the result of guilt over choosing the world we made (based on lack) over God's love, which is everything. The Course suggests to us that since we were created in love, and love is all there is, then true abundance is recognizing our true nature as Christ; the Son of God. In Heaven, there is no choice to be made, since our reality as part of God is just implied. At the level of the world where we believe we are, we need to choose Christ as our identity over the ego. Then, *The abundance of Christ is the natural result of choosing to follow Him.*[2] The key word here is choosing. It is our choice which teacher we choose to follow in our minds. Any symbols of abundance that show up in our scripts are just there to reflect our abundant state of mind. They are nothing in and of themselves. What matters is your state of mind, how kind and loving you are, and being of service to others.

Who is Christ? *You* are. Jesus knew this, too. He wasn't implying that he, alone, was the only Son of God. He knew that all of us as *one mind* are the Son of God. It is impossible for the Son of God to be in a state of lack, because we weren't created in lack. We were created in love, and therefore that is what we are. It is so common to feel lack that sometimes we don't realize when we are feeling it. It shows up in our relationships through the dynamic of projection. The ego uses our special relationships as substitutes for God's love. When we don't get something we want from our partners or they haven't fulfilled a role we assigned to them, we might get angry. The problem isn't our partners. The problem is the belief that our partners are responsible for our state of happiness. The part we forgot is that we wanted it that way.

To the ego, if we are helpless victims, it means we retain our innocence while our partners are the guilty ones that God is going to punish. Let's remember that this is unconscious to us. Bringing it to the surface can help us return to a miraculous state of mind where the choice for the Holy Spirit becomes obvious and desirable.

Being in a state of lack has become automatic to us, and so "normal" that something seems strange when everything seems to go our way. We might even say, "I can't believe I got that promotion!" Or, "I can't believe how well my relationship is going!" Under the surface we might even feel uncomfortable when good things happen to us, because unconsciously we don't feel we deserve it, but mostly, we believe we will lose it. So, we downplay our successes, even in our relationships, and when someone gives us a compliment, we have to make excuses for it, instead of just saying, "Thank you," and leaving it at that. That is guilt playing itself out.

In the holy relationship, there would be no need to use the relationship to serve the body in any way. This doesn't mean that we won't try. Also, it doesn't mean we won't have sex or have physical contact, which are normal things for bodies to do. It only means that we wouldn't *need* these things to feel whole. You can just join with your partner out of your mutual awareness of abundance. I've heard many Course students say that they have lost interest in many things, because the world is an illusion. The things they used to do feel pointless. Does this sound familiar? Gary and I feel that when you know the world is an illusion, it can actually make things even more exciting! If the ego doesn't have a grip on you anymore, because you remember you are dreaming, you can have more fun as things become less serious. This doesn't mean you don't have compassion or care about what is happening in the world or with other people. It means that regardless of what is happening, you retain your peace. When you've reached this point in your awareness, it can shift your special relationship into a holy one. There would be no need to project your unconscious guilt onto the other, because you would see that it hurts you to do that. As soon as you become aware, you see that it doesn't make sense anymore, and you will let it go.

As you can now see, abundance is a state of mind, and has nothing to do with the world. How can abundance come from a world that is based on lack, and furthermore is not even here? That's why it has nothing to do with anything material. The material world is not what makes you happy, even if you are successful according to the world's standards. You might have a great job that brings in a lot of money, a wonderful family, or be in a state of perfect health. There is nothing wrong with having success in the world, but you will further your spiritual progress if you don't take it too seriously. With true abundance, you will always have what you need *when* you need it, regardless of circumstances. It requires faith that you are given everything, because you were created as everything. I like to say, "The Holy Spirit has my back."

When you are in a relationship with someone, are you with that person because you *need* them, or because you *enjoy* being with them? If there is any feeling within you that says you are with this person in your life because they complete you, it falls into the "need" category. It's a cute idea, but in truth you don't need anyone else to complete you. When you feel complete within yourself you are a living example of abundance. Jesus understood that he came from what is whole, and that what is whole is filled with light. He remembered his identity as part of God. He was teaching we are all the same and equally loved by God. Therefore, we are equally whole with Him. I can't think of a better definition of living in abundance than investing our faith in that idea.

You experience the feeling of wholeness by cultivating your relationship with God. You can cultivate your relationship with God by identifying with Him through true prayer. *Seek ye first the Kingdom of Heaven, because that is where the laws of God operate truly, and they can operate only truly because they are the laws of truth.*[3] This requires trust that God's laws are operating for the highest good of all concerned. We don't even have to know what that is. Just trust. What it takes to get to a place of feeling abundant is a change of mind. It's changing the way you see now, which you can do by seeking or "willing" the Kingdom of Heaven first (which is what the quote above refers to) which will then inspire a different perception of yourself, others and your environment. A few questions to ask that might be helpful in staying vigilant only for God in regards to your personal relationships is "Where is my starting point when I have an interaction with someone? Am I at peace in my mind before I act? Who am I thinking with?" Remember, you can be the observer of yourself in action, and watch what you do without judgment.

You are constantly in a relationship with someone or something whether you realize it or not. When you are experiencing something, you can either choose to feel lack about it or abundant in relation to it. By training your mind to recognize the moments throughout your day when you feel lack, you can then be in a position to change your mind about it at that moment. These consistent moments of practicing every day will eventually cause a shift to take place within you, and the result is peace.

Back in the nineties, when I was in my twenties, I was infatuated with a guy that would not, (and could not), love me back, even though we were dating on and off. Looking back, I would say that he didn't treat me very well and tried to exploit me. At the same time, I was still so attracted to him that I allowed his behavior without confronting it. We did have fun and had many exciting times together, but in the bigger picture, it wasn't a very healthy relationship. Sometimes, I would show up for a dinner that he invited me to only to find out he wasn't there. At one point, I was so attached to him that I could think of nothing else. I was practicing the false kind of prayer, saying to God, "Please have him call me!" One day, I was feeling especially down about it, and I was lying in my bed when I suddenly felt a pair of hands on my shoulders. No one else was in the room. It was the most gentle and loving presence I had ever felt up to that point in my life. It felt like the hands of an angel. The hands were massaging my shoulders as if to say, "Relax. Everything will be okay. You are loved and taken care of." I really needed that assurance in that moment. I was so grateful for that experience and it helped me to know I was not alone.

Later, when I was introduced to the Course, and I recalled this experience, I was astounded when I read the following words: *Christ's hand has touched your shoulder, and you feel that you are not alone.*[4] That is exactly what I felt. The whole quote from this part of the Course is worthy of reciting here. I think some of you will relate to it if you have gone through something similar with a relationship, but started to feel there was another way of looking at it. It says, *Your ancient fear has come upon you now, and justice has caught up with you at last. Christ's hand has touched your shoulder, and you feel that you are not alone. You even think the miserable self you thought was you may not be your Identity. Perhaps God's Word is truer than your own. Perhaps His gifts to you are real. Perhaps He has not wholly been outwitted by your plan to keep His Son in deep oblivion, and go the way you chose without your Self.*[5] This passage is saying we are starting to see the light of truth dawn upon our minds, and that we are now beginning the process of including our true Self on our journey, with God as our goal. We are now opening our minds to the fact that we have been wrong about who we thought we were (the ego/body) and accepting our Christ nature.

Back to the story, when I felt the hands touch my shoulder, I had already been on a spiritual path for a few years. As a result of that, I was very open to having mystical experiences. This was the time I was having all kinds of out-of-body experiences and opening up to other realms in general. Eventually, when I started dating someone else, the guy in this story came around even more and tried to keep the relationship going, but by then it was too late. I had fallen in love with another guy (my former husband, Steve) and nothing could turn that around.

Note: I talk more about Steve in my second book, *The Business of Forgiveness.*

Furthermore, I realized that this other guy was helping me realize (unconsciously) that I didn't love myself, and through his behavior I learned to look at my own behavior and how I contributed to the dysfunctional relationship. This is an example of how feeling unfairly treated can lead to an important realization about oneself.

The Course says, *Beware of the temptation to perceive yourself unfairly treated.*[6] Feeling unfairly treated is an attempt by the ego to retain your innocence at the cost of someone else's guilt. If I am unfairly treated, it is implied that the other person should suffer the unfairness with me. There is only one mind. This is how the Course puts it: *You cannot crucify yourself alone. And if you are unfairly treated, he must suffer the unfairness that you see. You cannot sacrifice yourself alone. For sacrifice is total. If it could occur at all it would entail the whole of God's creation, and the Father with the sacrifice of His beloved Son.*[7]

You may be getting the idea by now that you can't believe one thing to be true about someone without including yourself as well. This is one of the key points in the Course. There *is* no one else, because there is no world. Applying this idea to your relationships will assist you in the transition from the special relationship to the holy one. In the holy relationship, you will still do the things you would normally do with each other, but it will be done with compassion, non-judgment, and a new type of freedom, where you free the other person to be as they are without trying to change them. What you change (if needed) is yourself. When you change, you will *experience* the "outer" circumstances differently, even if the specific person or events don't change. You may have shifted dimensions of time, but that is a topic for another time. Changing yourself might also bring external changes to the relationship for the better. I always let the Holy Spirit be in charge of that.

OLD IDEAS OF MONEY AND STATUS
IN RELATION TO ABUNDANCE

In addition to feeling lack in our relationships, a common area where people feel lack is around money. This can negatively affect your relationship if it's not dealt with. Since Gary and I get a lot of questions about money, I'd like to address it. Just like with people, we have a relationship with money. Lots of us create illusions that there is never quite enough money, even when you do have money. When your perception shifts around the energy of money from one of lack to reflecting the Holy Spirit's purpose for it, the *experience* you are having in relation to your financial situation will improve. Notice that I said the *experience* may shift, but not always the external situation, although it can. The Holy Spirit doesn't care how much money you have, but you can perceive money as a *symbol* of abundance without making it the only form of abundance in the world.

Even though abundance is a state of mind, there are a number of ways in which abundance can show up in the world as a reflection of an abundant state of mind. The symbol of abundance is not limited to money. It can show up as a gift given to you, an exchange or trade of some kind, something someone does for you that is meaningful to you, or something someone says to you that changes how you look at your life, to name of few. I'm using money as an example, because money is an issue in a lot of relationships.

If you are having problems with your partner about money, ask yourself what you feel your relationship with money is in this moment. What feelings come up when you think about money? Answering this question will tell you a lot about how you are looking at money and what it means to you. If you let money be used for the Holy Spirit's purpose, it will feel more purposeful and not just something you need to get for yourself. If you feel lack around money, recognize when you are feeling that way, which can be tricky because it's become an automatic response to feel this lack. When you do notice it, forgive yourself for feeling this way, remember your innocence, and tell yourself there is always enough, and that your source of strength and supply comes from God, not from little paper strips and metal discs. If you are one who has an abundance of money, you can also know that money is neither spiritual nor non-spiritual in its nature. It is neutral. The only thing that matters is the purpose it's serving. It's also okay to have nice things and celebrate. There is a lot of guilt around money, both in having a lot of money and not having it. Either way, the guilt can always be traced back to the idea that we felt we had true abundance in God's love, and threw it away, substituting illusions for truth. This can be forgiven like anything else. The following passage describes what appeared to happen when we made these substitutions:

> You who believe that God is fear made but one substitution. It has taken many forms, because it was the substitution of illusion for truth; of fragmentation for wholeness. It has become so splintered and subdivided and divided again, over and over, that it is now almost impossible to perceive it once was one, and still is what it was. That one error, which brought truth to illusion, infinity to time, and life to death, was all you ever made. Your whole world rests upon it. Everything you see reflects it, and every special relationship that you have ever made is part of it.[9]

If you think about the passage above in terms of your special relationships, it becomes clear that we've made just about everything into a special relationship, whether it is with people, money, substances, or things, with the ultimate special relationship being with the ego. These ideas are meant to be practiced at the mind level.

Coming back to the example about money, it doesn't mean you shouldn't take action or not do something about it if you find yourself financially depleted. However, the practice is forgiving any guilt you might be feeling about money. In relationships where you might be building a life with someone, if there is an emergency situation where you lost your job, or just aren't able to make ends meet, it would be very practical to do the best you can and seek financial assistance or help in some way. Remember, abundance can show up in different ways, not just around money. Practice not limiting yourself to the way in which your path may unfold. **Your worth is not equated with how much money you have**. It takes time to train the mind to think this way since a lot of us are taught that our self-worth is connected to our jobs and how much money we make for ourselves, partners, and our families.

A FORGIVENESS THOUGHT PROCESS REGARDING LACK

A forgiveness process around money might look something like this: *I realize that this experience has triggered thoughts of lack within me regarding money. It is only my thoughts that cause me any worry or feelings of lack, and nothing else. These are not my real thoughts. I am an innocent child of God and do not need anything outside of me to fulfill me; I have everything I need within me **now**. God is my source of strength and supply, and I trust in His Voice (the Holy Spirit) completely as the higher plan for me unfolds. I forgive myself for using this situation to make the separation real. I release this judgment upon myself and join with the Holy Spirit in peace.*

This general thought process can be used in any situation in your relationship where you feel lack by substituting another word for money. Another example of how lack shows up in relationships is around the issue of not receiving enough attention from your partner. You can use the above phrase, but the first sentence can say: *I realize that this experience has triggered thoughts of lack within me regarding the amount of time my partner and I spend together.* Then, continue with the exercise as stated above. This is a way of acknowledging what you are feeling without judgment, then forgiving yourself, which is recognizing your innocence. Remember, forgiveness is about letting go of the illusion of separation; that outside sources are not the cause of your upset because there is no outside. Our thoughts have not left the mind, so it is at the mind level that we want to make the shift.

Having a forgiveness thought process that you can practice consistently is what ultimately undoes the ego, but it is wise to practice every day. You will get so good at forgiveness that you may start to feel peaceful in situations in which you formerly felt discomfort. **Again, it is important to remember that it is only your thoughts that are the cause of pain, not the situation itself. It is how you interpret what you see that matters.** Usually, when one feels lack, it is because they are using the *past* as the light to guide them *now*. A key to feeling abundant is to be present and practice choosing the Holy Instant. To review, the Holy Instant is the instant you choose the miracle or forgiveness, which shifts your perception of yourself and what you believe to be your reality. More specifically, *In the holy instant, in which you see yourself as bright with freedom, you will remember God. For remembering Him* **is** *to remember freedom.*[9]

Coming back to abundance, one of the Workbook lessons in the Course that I use quite often to remind myself of abundance is this: *The past is over. It can touch me not.*[10] Remember, to the unconscious mind, the past is associated with sin (the idea of separation). We feel lack because we have moments that remind us or trigger this idea that we are separate from our Source. Of course, this is not true. You could never be separate from your Source because you are one with your Source. However, you can choose to believe you are separate, which can feel very real. To release the past (the idea of sin) and recognize that it is over, and in fact never happened in reality, induces an experience of being in the Holy Instant where you are whole, innocent and loved, which is being in a state of abundance. You are not only loved, you *are* love, and therefore only need to awaken to this fact. **When you are being love, you are being abundant.**

If you are coming from this kind of abundance in your relationships, the joy you will feel will be pure, and unpolluted by the poison of the ego that says you aren't enough or you aren't getting enough. Your happiness doesn't have to be determined by what someone does or doesn't do in your relationship. Thinking this way puts you at cause, where you can choose how you are interpreting things, rather than being at the effect, which is like being a puppet on a string, with the ego controlling it.

True abundance also leads to a deeper experience of intimacy, because real intimacy is about joining in the mind first, which can then take form in the most beautiful way. To use the example of sex, the act of sex itself does little to sustain the feeling of intimacy because it's a temporary feeling of gratification. To grow in intimacy is to appreciate the wholeness of your partner, and then "making love" becomes a way of joining out of a mutual state of appreciation for one another. Please don't misunderstand, I'm not saying that role-playing can't be fun once in a while, or that being outrageously spontaneous isn't exciting, rather I'm clarifying what it means to be in a state of true intimacy as opposed to just playing "romper room." I think it's time for a joke: A couple went to see a therapist and the therapist says, "So, tell me what brings you both here today?" Woman: "It's really difficult to live with him. He is so literal." Man: "My truck."

HOW LACK AROUND MONEY CAN AFFECT RELATIONSHIPS

Coming back to money for a moment (since it can often dominate a relationship depending on how it's used), one of the comments that I often receive from couples is that one person in the relationship is "wasting" money, inappropriately spending money, or completely mismanaging the money. These are different ways in which I hear this message. I think a lot of us have experienced some form of this. There is no doubt that this can lead to some pretty heavy arguments and hateful, vicious remarks, and even be cause for divorce. For some people, money means power, and it is how they define their worth. As long as this distorted sense of power remains, you will not get in touch with your real power, which has nothing to do with material things. There is nothing wrong with having money, or even wanting to have money, but there is nothing spiritual about it either. It is a neutral thing, and we put our own value onto it, making it what we want it to be. We give it all the meaning it has for us.

So, let's say that someone in the relationship is mismanaging money in some way. Since this mismanaging can take many forms, let's look at it in the larger context of not having a healthy relationship with money. When one doesn't have a healthy relationship with money, it's just a shadow/an effect of being in a state of lack. It would be wise in this case to start questioning what the deeper issues are in your mind that has caused the lack to take the form of money issues. One who does this is a good example of one who is going right to the cause rather than trying to fix what is on the screen, which is the effect. As with anything, it is ultimately for forgiveness.

When you take care of the mind first, the effect takes care of itself, and you will be guided as to the best solutions that may be helpful on the level of form. It takes willingness to look at it honestly and is also a way of taking responsibility for your mistakes. Mistakes shouldn't be cause for punishment, but should be acknowledged and then corrected. To correct your mistake, using this example, would be to correct your misperception of the purpose of the money. **When the Course talks about mistakes, it isn't talking about behavior, but mistakes in thinking. It's a Course in mind training, not behavior.**

Perhaps money has been used to serve the ego's purpose, rather than being given to the Holy Spirit to use for His purposes, which would produce a different experience. To use money for the Holy Spirit's purpose is to say: *Holy Spirit, please help me to perceive money* *correctly, and use it for **your** purposes for the highest good of all concerned.* When you give your money to the Holy Spirit in this way, it can be used as a helpful tool to use in whatever way enhances your growth, talents, and relationships.

If the issue around money takes the form of careless spending when you are not doing your part in bringing in any money, and it's putting the family in debt, it would be wise to take responsibility for your choices and question why you are using money in this way to fulfill an imagined need. In other words, your classroom is in session. Just going out and getting a job wouldn't necessarily solve the underlying issue unless you combined it with a willingness to look at the situation honestly, but also bring healing to the deeper issues going on in your mind that have been projected out in the form of money problems. This is taking care of the cause, and giving you the chance to bring long-term healing to it. The end result is one in which no matter what happens, you are still at peace. To not be willing to look at it and take responsibility is to be in a state of denial, but it is really a call for love. The Holy Spirit answers the call if you will accept His answer in place of yours.

This is not about making yourself guilty, but being the best version of yourself you can be by making a commitment to your spiritual growth, and using every challenge in your life as an opportunity to grow beyond it. This is a way of coming back to being empowered. **Remember, how much money you have doesn't define you or your worth. Your worth is established by God, and His judgment is always the same…you are innocent and His holy Son. The ego set it up so that money has power and worth. It can certainly buy you things in this world, but it cannot buy you happiness.**

Most of us want to be acknowledged and feel like we matter to other people. We don't want to be forgotten. I remember a time when I was about 7 or 8 years old. I went into my dad's office room and approached him at his desk. I took a piece of paper and I wrote the following words on the paper: *Remember me.* Then I handed him the piece of paper. To this day, I think he might still have that same piece of paper somewhere! He said he kept it for many years. I had some unconscious reason for writing that little note, but I believe part of it was about the importance for me to be "known" by him, not understanding that ultimately it was to be known by God. I do remember that note having quite an impact on him at the time, and even in my later years he'd bring it up and tell me he never forgot about it. That always brought a smile to my face, and it still does. I am so blessed to have such a loving and supportive father, and I appreciate him so much. My dad is a relatively "simple" man in terms of physical needs, and brilliant. The simplicity of his nature is what I admire most about him. Not only is he very intelligent, but he's humble. He enjoys the simple things in life, such as taking walks in nature, looking up at the night sky, watching the birds in his backyard, and tending to the garden. He is also very active in his community, always working for the higher good. I think the simplicity rubbed off on me, and I'm grateful for that.

It is always nice to be acknowledged, and it would be great if we could just leave it at that. What happens is that the need to be acknowledged grows into the burden of worrying about what other people think about us, especially in the special relationship. This is an exhausting way to live, and blocks our real thoughts from coming through. Why does it matter so much to us to gain acceptance from other people? A part of us is still looking outside ourselves for love, validation, and acceptance where it cannot be found. Again, the ego chose to believe that God's love wasn't enough for us, so we made special relationships as a substitute for God's love. We put all our faith in these special relationships instead of where it really belongs, in God. Isn't this what being poor really means? When you don't have God, you feel poor; not always consciously, but definitely unconsciously. In truth, we are all rich beyond our wildest dreams because we are an extension of God's love! All we need to do is accept that thought in our minds and then share and extend that thought to others. **Sharing is the root of all Creation**.

When you take the ideas of true abundance and start applying them to your relationships,

you will experience many more moments of what I like to call *true presence* with your partner. **True Presence is when no thought of the past or future interferes to block authentic communication with one another and hold you to the past, or tempt you to have expectations about the future.** You will see your partner for the first time without any stories attached to them, or even any future ideas. In this state, you can give and receive fully, and be in a state of Grace with your partner, where all judgments dissolve, and your thoughts are pure. In other words, you are really "seeing" the essence of love in your partner, thinking about them as they really are in truth. This is spiritual sight. I can't think of a better way to experience intimacy with your partner than to be in true presence. If your partner is open, practice being in true presence with each other, if you sense an argument brewing. A few minutes in this state can wash away years of judgment, condemnation, and the feeling of being unfairly treated. Over time, you will experience dramatic results in your ability to give and receive love.

If you find yourself forgetting to practice forgiveness or to do the exercises you've committed to do each day, just be aware that it's the resistance of the ego, and that is the ego's job; it wants you to forget. The ego knows that the undoing of it means the end of its existence. That is very fearful. It's best to just look at the thought within you and admit that it says, "I don't want to do this work," then let go of judgment, and trust that you will accept the love of the Holy Spirit when you are ready. You can do this with any judgmental thought. If you find yourself making yourself guilty for it, try practicing a forgiveness thought process to replace the ego's thoughts. Then, let it go. The Holy Spirit will take care of the rest.

PAGE FOR PERSONAL NOTES

CHAPTER 8

REALITY AS CO-CREATING WITH GOD

For God and His beloved Son do not think differently. And it is the agreement of Their thought that makes the Son a co-creator with the Mind Whose Thought created him.[1]

C o-creating in the truest sense is the oneness you share with God. In our personal relationships, co-creating can take different forms to reflect the true joining in Heaven. I mentioned in the last chapter that sharing is the root of all creation. God, in His love for you, His one Son, shares His love for you by extending it and sharing everything He is, while holding you in the perfect oneness of creation. God willed His Son to create and share, giving His Son the exact same ability to create; thus are you co-creators. Since God is love, real creation can only *be love.*

From this place of understanding, think of your partner as co-creator with you, in the name of love. What you can create together is a reflection of the one true Creation in Heaven. Join with your partner in your mind each day, recognizing that he or she is exactly the same as God in reality, just like you are. This is what it means to extend love, to co-create. There is no male or female in Heaven, which is perfect oneness. At the level of the world, this takes the form of having shared interests. You are not apart. Everything you perceive about your partner can become a reflection of the truth. When you get into an argument with your partner, the ideas above can help to bring you back to the ultimate truth. If you are already in the middle of a heated argument, it's easy to forget it. You can come back to the truth later, when you think of it, and still do the inner work. Since there is no time, your efforts will still have a positive impact on the relationship. The Holy Spirit takes your little willingness to forgive and applies it where it needs to go. You don't have to think about the outcome of the gift of forgiveness you give to your partner (or anyone). Let the Holy Spirit handle the results. All you need to do is recognize when the ego has dominated your decision-making, and choose again.

When you think about creating in partnership with your loved one, recognize that it is the love and intention behind it that is real and important. The form does not matter. The idea is to join with your partner and share in the blessings of your union. At the level of the world, creation can take the form of specific things you can create together. If it is infused with love, then it will be a reflection of true creation in Heaven. So, you can get in touch with the essence of what it is you want to create. Even if it's something on the level of form, is it love that is inspiring the action? Take a moment to ponder these questions: What does creating with your partner mean to you? What purpose does it serve? What value does it hold?

Any resistance that may come up with this idea of co-creating is only the ego wanting to maintain the separation, keeping its specialness intact, and making differences real. You can let that go and release it into the light of truth. If there is no resistance, then rejoice in the feeling of connectedness you share with your partner in the presence of your Creator. Visualize or imagine bringing your creation into fruition in a spirit of joining, love, and partnership. Feel the joy it brings you with every fiber of your being. It is only in the sharing of it that makes it meaningful. Be grateful for the gift you are giving to each other, and for the blessing this gift offers. You are blessed because you have chosen to create in the spirit of your Creator. Thank Him for endowing you with the same ability to create or to extend love. There is nothing else you have to do. Trust that the Holy Spirit will guide you in your endeavors, knowing that all is taken care of. All is calm, and all is well.

Part of this was taken from the meditation on co-creating, from our *Meditations for Couples* CD. The underlying principle in co-creating is always the understanding that love is the driving force of any co-creation. If it is inspired by love, it is coming from truth. To paraphrase the Course, when we are not thinking with God, we become depressed, since we are not extending God's love. The sadness comes when we are resisting God's love, not fulfilling our function as co-creator with God, and are therefore depriving ourselves of joy. The Course says, *Your ego and your spirit will never be co-creators, but your spirit and your Creator will always be.*[2]

We know couples who love co-creating together in the name of love, and are well-intentioned, but often misinterpret it to mean that they should do absolutely everything together all the time and be interested in every single thing their partner does, because that means they love them. It makes the form real. Examples might include going to painting classes together, even if one partner doesn't find painting exciting; watching every movie together, even if the other isn't interested in the subject matter; eating the same kinds of food, even if the other prefers a different diet. In other words, it's a misunderstanding that you have to do everything your partner wants to do, which is often at the expense of neglecting your own personal interests. This behavior isn't coming from love if you aren't being honest with yourself, and it falls into the category of sacrifice. This is an important subject, because lots of arguments and impatience in relationships comes from both people not really honoring the fact that the other has an individual path/curriculum, in addition to what they share together. Feelings of frustration and even resentment can build up over time if one isn't careful to honor one's own natural interests. This is not to be confused with specialness. It just honors the awareness that we all have preferences and personal choices. It's okay to say, "I prefer to do this today, thank you." So, if you find yourself in a situation where you are not honoring yourself in this way, please give yourself this gift.

Relationships grow, thrive, and can become even more intimate when both people allow the other to have his or her breathing space when needed, and in some cases even taking a weekend or short time apart if that's what is needed. It's really okay to do this. Being apart, even for just a short time may give you clues as to how dependent you've really become on your partner for so many things, and may even feel uncomfortable for a time. One reason for this is that many of us feel uncomfortable being by ourselves, or without our partners. If we are by ourselves, we tend to look inward more, and there is great resistance to the silence of looking inward. Many of us can't turn the noise off, which can take the form of having the TV on all day, the radio playing in the background, or constant talking on the phone, or being on our computers, texting, and the list goes on and on. Again, being in the silence and not doing anything is just too much to bear for the ego. We seek for love outside of ourselves, and forget that the love we are seeking is not only what we are, but right here now, within us.

Some of us may have also realized, or have probably said at some point in our lives, "I've noticed that when I'm not with my partner, I appreciate them more." The feeling of "missing" our partners can make us realize how much we do enjoy being with them, having a new sense of appreciation. This can be a beautiful thing if it's not confused with possessiveness or neediness and can help the relationship grow in exciting ways. There is something intriguing and attractive about the idea that your partner has a life of his or her own, in addition to the one they share with you. It keeps things fresh and interesting. So, I recommend it.

As I said before, Gary and I spend most of our 24 hours together, since we live, work, and share our lives together. We love each other very much, and it works for us. We do have our own interests, too, and there are times when I'm not able to travel with Gary, but we both seem to notice that after being a part for a time, we come back together with an extra boost of excitement and appreciation, as well as gratitude that we found each other in the first place. It's a very nice, rewarding feeling. We do miss each other when we are apart for a longer period of time, but we realize that it's just the separation playing itself out in that form.

Wouldn't it be nice to come to the place in your relationship where you could just allow the other person the freedom to be who they are? The need for possessiveness just falls away. In other words, honoring and respecting each other's natural expression to come through without judgment. That is a beautiful idea. Love doesn't limit anyone or anything. If frees the other person to be as they are. Love is just itself. It doesn't have to do anything. **You *are* love, you don't *do* love.** When we are being love, we don't have to fix the screen or change other people/the outer picture. The intervention we are always hoping for someone else is really for us. We need to intervene in our own lives, which starts in our own minds, where the cause is. Sometimes it's harder to do in certain situations. It's during these times that we develop the understanding that it's our own pain and not someone else's that we need to deal with. You are worth the consistent effort to keep building respect for yourself, not having someone else prove they can be respectful to you. There is no one else "out there" to prove anything. In building your spiritual house from within, love will be there and guide you with the steps to take (if any) that are in alignment with your inner efforts. Ultimately, the outer picture tends to take care of itself when the inner picture is nurtured. The final exercise is to trust that it is being taken care of and things will be okay.

A COMMON QUESTION ABOUT
THE ILLUSORY WORLD

There have been quite a few Course people in our workshops who ask the following, common question: "If the world is an illusion, bodies are not real, and there is only one of us, why have children?" In order to answer this question, it would be helpful to remember that the Course is given on two levels, the metaphysical/spiritual level and the level of the world. The Course doesn't say anything about having to give up things in the world, or that you shouldn't have children while you appear to be here. It does, however, guide us to give up the ego as our teacher, and turn to the Holy Spirit instead. It's about changing your mind about the world and how you are looking at everything, including bodies. If you pro-create, it would be nice if your underlying intention is to co-create by extending the perfect love of your Creator to your children. As long as we all have lessons we are learning here, dreaming these bodies can be viewed as a helpful tool for us to learn our lessons of forgiveness and return to God.

I remember a friend of ours saying to us, "I feel a little uncertain about having children, because it seems that lots of advanced spiritual teachers don't have children. What's the point if it's all an illusion anyway?" We always answer this question the same way: Having children doesn't mean you are not spiritually advanced. Many spiritually advanced people have children. Perhaps there are lessons being learned that are helping each one in the family progress along their spiritual path. No one can judge what is best for another person. Having children is a personal choice, and if it feels guided, then it can still serve the Holy Spirit's purpose. We were all children once, so it would be kind of silly to say that others shouldn't have children because the world is an illusion. Always ask the Holy Spirit for guidance about these matters.

Part of what we are learning here is to share the perfect love of God. As the ego is gradually undone, fewer bodies will appear to be here, because more people will become enlightened, making the illusory experience of reincarnation unnecessary. *And the closer you get to enlightenment, the attraction of bodies diminishes,* as Pursah describes in *Love Has Forgotten No One.* She also says, *If you or your partner feel guided to have children, you should have children. There is a reason for that, and it has to do with the interlocking chain of forgiveness.* You can see from Pursah's comment that there is an Atonement plan, and for some it involves having children. Just pay attention to what part of you wants to have children, and if it feels authentic and loving, coming from of place of wanting to share your love, that is wonderful. Try not to let the idea of the illusion stop you from doing "normal" things in the world. It would be like saying, "Since the world is an illusion, I won't have any pets, because that would mean that I'm making bodies real, and I don't want to be a bad Course student." Furthermore, there is not one form/body that is more important than another.

The Course expresses the idea that mind is mind, and it doesn't matter what the container appears to be. To say that some species should be treated differently than others is to play the specialness game and to make a hierarchy out of illusions; one species is greater or more worthy of our attention than others, when the Course is saying that none of it's real, because there is no life outside of Heaven. If none of it is real, why would one form of body be better or more important than another form? Also, it is true that different species appear to have different degrees of advancement. That doesn't mean those species that may be more advanced are any better or more worthy than others. We don't look at people and say, that person over there is more advanced spiritually, and therefore that means I don't really matter and have no purpose here. We understand that everyone here is growing and learning lessons with the ultimate goal of awakening in God. That is why we are the same. We share the same goal. We are co-creators with each other and with God when we are extending the all-inclusive nature of God's love.

Regarding other species, it has been said that our Cetacean community, such as the dolphins, are more advanced than we are, and I really don't see any evidence that would contradict that. When Gary and I swam with the dolphins in Hawaii, we sensed we weren't more advanced than they were. In fact, I had complete respect for them and their ability to telepathically communicate, which is a highly developed skill they have. Humans will start to move in that direction as well, eventually being in telepathic communication with each other and other species on a continuous basis. We can be in co-creation with many different beings, as I've described in my other books, but if we don't accept them as our brothers and sisters, it will take much longer to make contact with them in any meaningful way.

Back to children for a moment, Gary and I established early on in our relationship that, although we enjoy children, neither of us felt guided to have children. Our chosen career paths don't make it any easier, since our careers include extensive traveling. Perhaps that's why we decided to get Luna, our beautiful cat. She is such a joy to be around and has such an expressive personality. She is our baby, and we are lucky to have such a wonderful arrangement for her when we leave town. Sometimes, she stays at her Aunt Jackie and Uncle Mark's house when we're out of town, and she loves it there. One of the reasons she loves it there is because she is the reincarnation of my sister Jackie's former cat, Murphy. So, Luna recognizes her former surroundings and all of us as her extended family. That was clear at the beginning when we first saw her. She immediately took to us, and it was as if we'd been together for a long time. Then, we found out that Luna has been incarnating in our family off and on for centuries. Animals do that, just like people. They come back to be with you, and play different roles.

I asked Spirit once, "Do dogs sometimes incarnate as cats, and do cats come back as dogs?" Spirit said, "Yes, but a cat will never admit it." Those that have cats might also relate to the following statement that I saw on a greeting card I received from a friend: "Ask not what your cat can do for you, ask what you can do for your cat." It is also true that cats always have the best seat in the house. I think they know they are Gods. In ancient Egypt they were seen as Gods. I'm not playing favorites here as I love *all* animals. I've had dogs as companions, too, and they are also so easy to love.

The reason I bring all this up is not to make bodies real. On the level of form, it keeps things fun and light, so that everything doesn't have to be taken so seriously and feel so heavy. We can live the happy dream of forgiveness and lighten up a bit! Animals are our brothers, too, as well as our friends in space (the E.T.'s). The idea of co-creation can extend to *all* beings, whether on this planet or others. Besides, wouldn't our experience of life here be kind of boring without animals or other types of beings? Animals in particular are masters of entertainment, and they enhance our life experiences. They can share and extend love in miraculous ways, such as rescuing people from dangerous situations or showing their respect and appreciation as they mourn a loved one's passing. There are countless stories of compassion and interaction between humans and animals, as well as between one particular animal species and another. They also understand the *true presence* idea I spoke of in an earlier chapter. Thank you, our dear animals. We love you.

For those of you who have read my other books, you know that I love to talk about animals and E.T.'s. Part of my script is to learn and teach through communication with other types of beings. It's also a hobby of mine. Each of us has our personal scripts with our own hobbies, but there is a difference between the *form* our personal life scripts take and the higher curriculum of learning and understanding about our reality. This is what the Course says about that:

> *This is a course in miracles. It is a required course. Only the time you take it is voluntary. Free will does not mean that you can establish the curriculum. It means only that you can elect what you want to take*

at a given time. The course does not aim at teaching the meaning of love, for that is beyond what can be taught. It does aim, however, at removing the blocks to the awareness of love's presence, which is your natural inheritance. The opposite of love is fear, but what is all-encompassing can have no opposite.[3]

We need to learn through our special relationships, no matter what form they take, that the goal is to transcend them. Having an intimate relationship involves undoing the ego so that true intimacy becomes your experience. The blocks we are removing are the attack thoughts and judgments that come from unconscious guilt. The more we make the shift from the ego mind to the Holy Spirit, the holy relationship will be the result. Any being you are in contact with can help serve the purpose of being truly helpful in a way that deepens your personal relationships, specifically the romantic ones, depending on what purpose you are letting all your relationships serve.

Earlier in this chapter, I mentioned a meditation on co-creating in your relationship. I'd like to include it here so those of you who are currently in a romantic relationship can practice. The content in this meditation can be applied to *any* relationship by just tweaking some of the words to reflect your particular situation. Also, the creating I am speaking of here is meant to reflect your true creation in Heaven. We need to use symbols here since we are still experiencing ourselves in the world. With that in mind, enjoy the following meditation.

MEDITATION ON CO-CREATING
IN YOUR RELATIONSHIP

Think of your partner as co-creator with you. What you create together in the name of love is a reflection of the one, true creation in Heaven. Join with your partner in your mind, recognizing that they are exactly the same as you in reality. There is no male or female in Heaven, which is perfect oneness. At your core, you have shared interests. You are not apart. Everything you perceive about your partner is a reflection of what is in your own mind.

Visualize or imagine something you would like to create together. It could be building a new house, starting a family, starting a new business, having a more loving relationship, better communication, or whatever it is that is meaningful to you now. As you think of what it is you want to create, recognize that it is the love and intention behind it that is real and important. The form does not matter. The idea is to join with your partner and share in the blessings of your union. Get in touch with the essence of what it is you want to create. Take a moment to ponder these questions: What does manifesting it mean to you? What purpose does it serve? What value does it hold?

Breathe slowly and deeply. Any resistance that may come up is only the ego wanting to maintain the separation, and wanting to keep its own existence intact. You can let that go and release it into the Light of Truth. If there is no resistance, then rejoice in the feeling of connectedness you share with your partner in the presence of your Creator. Visualize or imagine bringing your creation into fruition in a spirit of joining, love, and partnership. Feel the joy it brings you with every fiber of your being. It is only in the sharing of it that makes it meaningful. Be grateful for the gift you are giving to each other, and for the blessing this gift offers. You are blessed because you have chosen to create in the spirit of your Creator. Silently, thank your partner for joining with you during this time. Thank your Creator for endowing you with the same ability to create or extend love.

There is nothing else you have to do. Trust that the Holy Spirit will guide you in your endeavors, knowing that all is taken care of. All is calm, and all is well...God Is. (End of meditation)

When I think of what Gary and I have co-created together, I think of our journey with the Course and helping each other along the path home. We have difficulties in our scripts just like everyone else. We also have to do the inner work. In the world, we have certainly created many things together, but we have worked on the understanding that the creations that involve spiritual growth are the most meaningful. I hope the following questions that I have asked at various points in my relationship with Gary will be helpful to you as well: Are we truly communicating as opposed to answering to the ego's desires? Are we forgiving those things in our relationship that have disturbed our peace? Do we come together in support of one another during times of challenge? Do we practice non-judgment and allow each other to be him or her self? Do we respect the idea of having our own path as well as the path we share together as a couple? Are we inspired to grow and learn together, taking our relationship to new heights?

Asking the above questions can help you to stay on track and cultivate true intimacy with your partner as long as these questions are sincerely pondered and discussed. Authenticity and honesty are important in having successful relationships. Sometimes, even if only one person in the relationship is wholly forgiving and perceiving correctly, the relationship can still thrive. This is not always the case, but it can happen. If you are in a relationship with someone and it's not going well, you might just be in a phase where you are being guided to look deeper at what is most important to you. It doesn't mean your relationship has to end. There is no such thing as a perfect relationship. There will be bumps along the way, but those bumps don't have to become boulders if you stay mindful on a daily basis. Everything has its time, including the time when you feel ready to really look at the things in your relationship that are bothering you. Try not to beat yourself up if you feel you should have looked sooner. The fact that you may be looking now means you are ready; it is your time.

All of the things that happen in our lives are leading us to specific points in our scripts where we are given the opportunity to pause, reflect, and makes shifts and changes, if necessary. I often think of the following passage in the Course when a challenge comes up:

Have you really considered how many opportunities you have had to gladden yourself, and how many of them you have refused? There is no limit to the power of a Son of God, but he can limit the expression of his power as much as he chooses. Your mind and mine can unite in shining your ego away, releasing the strength of God into everything you think and do. Do not settle for anything less than this, and refuse to accept anything but this as your goal. Watch your mind carefully for any beliefs that hinder its accomplishment, and step away from them. Judge how well you have done this by your own feelings, for this is the one right use of judgment.[4]

The depth of what this statement means goes right to the heart of the Course's teaching on the power to choose, as well as the determination and willingness it takes to be vigilant *only* for God. You might find that re-reading this passage often will help you to stay determined to *not* let the special relationship with the ego bring you down. Part of this is saying that your feelings will tell you which teacher you have chosen to be your guide. I have already spoken on the importance of paying attention to your feelings. It is another tool you can use to help you shift to another way of seeing. The Workbook of the Course also helps us to shift the way we see now to a new understanding of what it means to see with true Vision.

True Vision in the Course has nothing to do with the body's eyes. It has to do with looking past form (making the body real) to the reality of the Christ in each of us (our true identity). This can be applied to your relationships by practicing true Vision every day, regardless of what is happening or what things look like. Whether you stay in a relationship or leave one, you can still practice making the foundation of your life one that stays connected to the truth. You are one with everyone and everything. *Oneness is simply the idea God is. And in His Being, He encompasses all things. No mind holds anything but Him. We say "God is," and then we cease to speak, for in that knowledge words are meaningless.*

There are no lips to speak them, and no part of mind sufficiently distinct to feel that it is now aware of something not itself. It has united with its Source. And like its Source Itself, it merely is.[5]

It doesn't hurt to come back to pure non-dualism, which is implied in the above statement. This book is about helping people stay on track with the truth, but using the special relationship to motivate you to choose again what you would have your reality be, along with your partner. It's this change of mind that allows the Holy Spirit to enter and use your relationship for His purposes, which allows it to become a holy relationship. We will take this a step further in the next chapter, deepening the idea of the holy relationship being the result of a right-minded one.

PAGE FOR PERSONAL NOTES

CHAPTER 9

THE RIGHT-MINDED
RELATIONSHIP

*Right-mindedness listens to the Holy Spirit, forgives the world, and
through Christ's vision sees the real world in its place.*[1]

When I think about the romantic relationships I've had over the
years, none of them were completely right-minded. It doesn't
mean there weren't wonderful moments and lots of laughter and joy,
but my point is that no relationship is really right-minded all the time
until you no longer need the relationship to serve the ego's purpose.
As the quote at the top of the page says, one would need to see the real
world in place of a world where separation and attack are still valued.
The real world is still part of the illusion, but it's a world that is seen
through the eyes of forgiveness.

I remember many times in relationships where I felt like a victim.
It's easy to be a victim, but not so easy to forgive. However, once you
start to feel the benefits of forgiveness and really stick to it, you might
be surprised to find out that forgiveness can be easier. Conflict is hard.
With conflict you have to prove you are right, which requires that you
build a defense. This can be exhausting, and reinforces the separation.

Forgiveness just requires a change of mind. It can take time to fully forgive, but with practice and patience, and a desire for peace above all else, you will do it. It will get easier with practice. Jesus says we need to have the conviction that we will succeed. The mind is very powerful. In fact, it's so powerful it can make up a false universe that seems very real. Imagine using the power of our minds to think with the Holy Spirit and remember God. That power can move mountains.

In the special relationships of the world, attack, which comes from fear, is very much valued as a defense mechanism against the guilt one feels inside. Once this guilt is healed, which is done through true forgiveness, the relationship will no longer need to serve the purpose of the ego. This means you are joining with another out of your mutual awareness of abundance. I've heard some people in the Course community say that you should leave all your special relationships. In other words, just abandon them. That is not what the Course is encouraging us to do. You won't be able to undo the unconscious guilt in the mind if you are running away from those relationships. We can't meditate away our guilt. It needs to be undone through practicing with the people and situations that really trigger us. The Holy Spirit doesn't want to take our special relationships away, but instead teach us how to transform them into holy ones.

The special relationship is part of our classroom where we learn what needs to be forgiven, which is ourselves for having made the separation real. The problem is that if the separation is real in our minds, the guilt that results from that belief will be projected onto the relationship. No one really escapes this at first. Once a person gets exhausted enough from all the conflict, that is a turning point where the person might say, "There has to be a better way." That is the invitation to the Holy Spirit to help you find that better way. We just have to be willing to receive and let go of our own ideas and assumptions of what things are supposed to look like. How could we know what the best outcome is for everyone involved?

A right-minded relationship is one where forgiveness and gratitude are cultivated. Being in a state of gratitude can assist in cancelling out any negative emotion you may be experiencing. It is also helpful to be grateful that you understand how the ego operates so you don't have to continue choosing it. You can end your days and be done with it, knowing you will sometimes make mistakes, but you don't have to dwell on those mistakes. Just let them go. Each day is a new chance to reinforce the right mind, and you can begin your days being so rich in Spirit that yesterday is simply forgotten.

I've always loved the following quote from Ralph Waldo Emerson, which can be helpful if you are in a conflicted relationship: "Finish each day and be done with it. You have done what you could. Some blunders and absurdities no doubt crept in; forget them as soon as you can. Tomorrow is a new day. You shall begin it serenely and with too high a spirit to be encumbered with your old nonsense." This is about letting go of the past, which is over, and accepting that today is a new opportunity to perceive things differently. Mistakes will be made, but they don't have to define you or another person. You can start each day so full of the Holy Spirit that it's not worth dwelling on what happened the day before. Remember the movie analogy? We are all watching a movie, like film strips that appear to be linear. If you think of yourself as just watching a series of images or frames from another level, you can remember that Jesus is right beside you (if you choose Him as your teacher) watching the movie with you. He can be your right-minded teacher that ignites the same ability within yourself to choose to think right-mindedly about everything.

One of my favorite lines in the Workbook of the Course is, *I loose the world from all I thought it was.*[2] You might want to use this line and imagine yourself loosening your partner from all you thought they were. In other words, letting go of all the false beliefs and ideas you might be holding about your partner, keeping them and yourself bound in chains. You see what you want to see in the world and in your special relationships. For clarity on this point, the Workbook lesson mentioned above says:

> *The world is nothing in itself. Your mind must give it meaning. And what you behold upon it are your wishes, acted out so you can look on them and think them real. Perhaps you think you did not make the world, but came unwillingly to what was made already, hardly waiting for your thoughts to give it meaning. Yet in truth you found exactly what you looked for when you came.*
>
> *There is no world apart from what you wish, and herein lies your ultimate release. Change but your mind on what you want to see, and all the world must change accordingly. Ideas leave not their source.*[3]

Later in this lesson it says:

> *But healing is the gift of those who are prepared to learn there is no world, and can accept the lesson now. Their readiness will bring the lesson to them in some form which they can understand and recognize. Some see it suddenly on point of death, and rise to teach it. Others find it in experience that is not of this world, which shows them that the world does not exist because what they behold must be the truth, and yet it clearly contradicts the world.*[4]

If the world does not exist, we don't either, at least not as bodies. Accepting that there is no world would save us all from a lot of unnecessary pain. However, for most of us it takes the illusion of time to fully accept the Atonement for ourselves. The value of being aware of the truth is that it can be applied to your life and relationships and save you time. Since you are an eternal being, there is no rush, but you also don't have to suffer. Sometimes we feel like we are suffering, and that can be a painful experience. In regards to this, I've always loved Jesus's uncompromising nature in the Course, especially when he says things like, *How can you who are so holy suffer? All your past except its beauty is gone, and nothing is left but a blessing. I have saved all your kindnesses and every loving thought you ever had. I have purified them of the errors that hid their light, and kept them for you in their own perfect radiance. They are beyond destruction and beyond guilt. They came from the Holy Spirit within you, and we know what God creates is eternal.*[5]

In order to experience what Jesus is talking about, it does require a change of mind. *If you are tempted to be dispirited by thinking how long it would take to change your mind so completely, ask yourself, "How long is an instant?" Could you not give so short a time to the Holy Spirit for your salvation?*[6] It doesn't have to take a long time, but it often does, because we've become so attached to the past and believe it offers us something we want. I'm always reassured when I read in the Course that the right-minded relationship is really about connecting with the Holy Spirit, the only holy relationship there is, and letting the love that comes from joining with the Holy Spirit be extended to include everyone.

As a reminder, in relationships there are always only two places to be coming from in our interactions with others: the right mind (Holy Spirit) or wrong mind (ego). **A holy relationship is a forgiven relationship, where each person allows the other the freedom to be who they are without judgment**. One has to be in one's right mind in order to practice forgiveness. The wrong mind judges and condemns. When anything upsets us or disturbs our peace, it is always because of some judgment we are holding about the person or situation, which is really a reflection of judgments we hold against ourselves. Also, we are never upset for the reason we think. Any time we are upset, in every case, it can always be traced back to the *tiny, mad idea* we talked about before, and that we actually took this idea that we could be separate from God seriously. This is why we are upset.

We think that it is something outside of us that causes us pain. Pain, no matter what the degree, is always the result of feeling cutoff from our Source, pretending to be someone or something we are not. *The ego is a wrong-minded attempt to perceive yourself as you wish to be, rather than as you are.*[7] What we are *not* is fear. What we *are* is love. If one could learn to identify with love, the fear would go away. Also, learn to notice what the judgments are and acknowledge them, moving into acceptance (not denying it happened), then forgive it, which would save countless fights and remove any unnecessary suffering.

A RIGHT-MINDED EXAMPLE OF RESPONDING TO CONFLICT

Here is an example: Let's say your partner starts yelling at you, projecting all their frustrations onto you because of a difficult day at work. This is a very common issue between couples. Your partner starts finding fault with you and seems to point out everything that you are doing wrong in the relationship and says that you need to change or else there will be consequences. They may be verbalizing countless things to you that may or may not be true. You may be thinking, "Where did this come from? I didn't do anything to deserve this treatment." Your temperature starts to rise, and you are beginning to feel the effects of the verbal attacks. You might even start yelling back, and on and on it goes until a full blown argument has ensued. It takes two to argue. It is still your responsibility how you choose to think about an issue and respond to it.

A right-minded way to handle this would be that you identify what the trigger was that started making you feel upset. In this case, the trigger was your partner's outburst or seeming attack against you. However, that is not the real reason you are upset. You wouldn't feel the slightest bit upset if you recognized it is *your* dream. If it is your dream, you wouldn't feel the need to react to it. In this scenario, you wouldn't be upset if a part of you didn't identify yourself as the being your partner is portraying as you. This means there is a belief you are holding about yourself that isn't true, but you responded as if it were true, defending your position. The truth is that both of you are not separate from God, and you are both the Christ/Son of God, completely innocent and invulnerable Spirit. The pain or hurt is felt when our thoughts about ourselves are not in alignment with our Christ selves. Giving our power away to others, which is giving people the power to make us feel happy, sad, angry, depressed, or whatever the emotion, is also upsetting. No one can make you happy or sad. It is a decision that you are making in your mind. Practice identifying the trigger, then looking at what the judgment is in your own mind. Then, acknowledge that you are feeling upset, and remember to apply forgiveness. It's okay if you don't feel you are in a proper place in your mind to do it right away. **You can give yourself a "pass" every now and then, but just know that the sooner you can forgive, the less you suffer.**

As you train your mind to automatically remember this process, remember that it is about *you*. No matter what the other person is saying to you, what you do is work on your own process, not try to change your partner. You might say to your partner, "I realize you are upset and now I'm feeling upset, too. I'd like to talk to you when I am feeling centered and in a place of peace. It seems that you are feeling this way, too. I want you to know that I love you very much, and I want to communicate with you. I know that if I take some time to center myself and turn this over to Spirit, I will feel much better."

Next, you can silently forgive yourself and your partner, not because both of you did something wrong, but because you thought of yourself and your partner as guilty, acting as a witness for the ego. All of this is only a mistake that needs correction. You might say in your mind, "I forgive myself for judging myself as guilty, which cannot be an idea God holds of me. I forgive myself for judging my partner as being a jerk, which is not his or her true self. Only love is real. I now join with the Holy Spirit in peace."

By the way, people can certainly *act* like jerks, but it doesn't mean they are really a jerk. If someone is acting like a jerk, they are just calling out for love. The following forgiveness exercise is worth repeating: *You're not really there. If I think you are guilty or the cause of the problem, and if I made you up, then the imagined guilt and fear must be in me. Since the separation from God never occurred, I forgive "both" of us for what we haven't really done. Now there is only innocence, and I join with the Holy Spirit in peace.* You can try communicating in the moment with your partner, but I recommend waiting until both of you are in a more centered, calm place. Sometimes, you may be the one practicing forgiveness and your partner is not. That is okay because all that is required is that you do your own inner work. It only takes one in the relationship to see right-mindedly and to practice forgiveness, and there will be benefits. Whoever is saner at the time can be inspired to practice forgiveness, doing their part, no matter what the other is doing. Trust that if there is something that would be truly helpful for you to do, the Holy Spirit will guide you.

Note: Even though it only takes one person to practice forgiveness in a relationship, it is still wise for both people involved to work at it. If they don't, conflicts may continue and the relationship may not reach its full potential. In other words, the more both people in the relationship are putting in effort, chances are that it will be a long-lasting, healthy relationship.

Our relationships are specifically chosen by us at another level, because there is something to learn from them, or some kind of healing that needs to take place; issues that are being resolved. It is a blessing even though it doesn't always seem that way. Just as one becomes a great pianist by practicing every day, one also becomes great at forgiveness when it is practiced every day. Experiencing a peaceful state of mind is worth it, is it not? Decide what kind of teacher you want to be for your partner. Do you want to add something positive, or fuel the fire by engaging in the same kind of thinking that started the argument? Whatever you choose is what you are teaching.

HOW TO CHANGE YOUR MIND
AND REMEMBER THE TRUTH

Remember, your partner may have countless accusations he or she holds against you, but there is really just one seeming problem, which can be manifested in countless forms. Any time the ego attacks, no matter what the form is of the attack, it has chosen the separation over union with God. Any time the ego responds to attacks in the form of attack, it is the same thing. One of my favorite sections in the Course is the chapter called *The Healing of the Dream*.[8] In the section, *The Hero of the Dream*,[9] there is a wonderful summary of what all this boils down to, and it is this:

> *The secret of salvation is but this: That you are doing this unto your-self. No matter what the form of the attack, this still is true. Whoever takes the role of enemy and of attacker, still is this the truth. Whatever seems to be the cause of any pain and suffering you feel, this is still true. For you would not react at all to figures in a dream you knew that you were dreaming. Let them be as hateful and as vicious as they may, they could have no effect on you unless you failed to recognize it is your dream.*[10]

> *This single lesson learned will set you free from suffering, whatever form it takes. The Holy Spirit will repeat this one inclusive lesson of deliverance until it has been learned, regardless of the form of suffering that brings you pain.*[11]

That is the part of the Course that I read to myself whenever I am tempted by the ego to choose wrong-minded thinking. It puts me right back in my place and helps me to choose again what I want my reality to be. We do not have to fear the ego, and just as we made it by investing our belief in it, we can undo it by withdrawing our belief in it. As an exercise, think of something in your relationship that really bothers you or a situation where you are tempted to blame your partner for how you feel. Then, practice what the passage above is saying. Forgive yourself if you feel you aren't ready to go all the way with it.

To re-emphasize some valuable points, the right-minded relationship takes lots of practice,

but it is in the practicing that you are growing into this kind of relationship. This is how you get there. In order to experience this kind of relationship, it requires that you first admit that, unconsciously, the ego part of you wants it to be difficult so that it can feel justified in being upset. Making the whole thing real is the ego's game plan. We make it real by making it our partner's fault when we become upset. We want it this way so we don't have to take responsibility for our part in choosing the separation. Instead, we blame our partners so that we can be the innocent victims. So, the first step is being aware that this is going on, and that it is the ego's plan. Once this has been identified, you can remember that there is another plan, and it's the Holy Spirit's plan. The Holy Spirit sees our projections without believing in them. To trust in the Holy Spirit's plan is to choose the Holy Spirit as your teacher instead of the ego. So, when something comes up in your relationship that is challenging you, ask yourself… how would the Holy Spirit look at this? If it's the Holy Spirit you are choosing to interpret the situation with, you will look through the eyes of non-judgment, without condemnation, and remember who that person really is, thinking the kinds of thoughts that God or the Holy Spirit would think. If God is love, there would be no thought that could contradict His love. The key here is remembering that since there is only one of us, any thoughts you are thinking about another person are really going to you.

What I am speaking of is something you can do at the mind level. I realize there are some situations where you may have to take some form of action in the relationship in order for it to move forward. This is not about not doing anything. No matter what you do, you can always think right-minded ideas during the process. Whenever you are tempted to condemn someone else, remind yourself that you are just condemning yourself since there is only one mind. The ego will always try and tempt you to think otherwise, but whatever teacher you choose will be an indicator of where you've invested your faith in that moment. None of this is about punishment, only correction. It's about correcting your misperceptions of who you think you are.

Another aspect of a right-minded relationship is being aware if you are placing your partner in a position that is beyond correction, or beyond forgiveness. When you are aware of it, you can do something to correct it. How many times have you heard people say, and maybe you are one of them: "I will never forgive them for what they have done, because what they did is unforgivable. They don't deserve my forgiveness." Underneath these words are a lot of painful feelings that are really saying, "I can't forgive *myself*. What *I've* done is unforgivable. I don't deserve to be forgiven. I am guilty and deserved to be punished." Unconsciously, we then punish ourselves by not forgiving ourselves, which allows the guilt to remain intact. Eventually, the guilt will get projected outward, and the cycle continues.

Someone once said, "To forgive is to set a prisoner free and discover that the prisoner is you." We are only hurting ourselves by not forgiving another. No one is beyond forgiveness. No exceptions. If we say someone is beyond forgiveness, it's the same thing as saying "I am beyond forgiveness." When this idea is really understood, you will be free. When you stop caring about what people think of you (even if they appear to judge you) you will be free. When you are practicing this mindset, you are thinking right-mindedly and reinforcing right-minded relationships.

GAINING CLARITY ON YOUR
ROLE IN YOUR RELATIONSHIP

To bring even more clarity to where you stand in the relationship, ask yourself what your role is in the relationship. Be clear on your role. This will help you to be less confused when you have choices to make that appear to be more challenging. Maybe your role is to be as loving and supportive as you can be with your partner, but not an enabler of egoic habits. Maybe it's to remain a spouse, instead of playing the role of a mother or father in the relationship. It is very easy to slip into a role where we start acting as if we are our partner's parent. There is nothing wrong with playing this role, but I doubt it will bring either you or your partner happiness. To be able to step back and let our partners choose for themselves without stepping in and trying to correct something they said or did, is to teach them that they have a mind, and they have the right to choose with their wrong or right mind. If we try to take that away from them, we are teaching them that they can't trust their own power to choose for themselves, which isn't a loving thing to do. We don't have to agree with what they are saying or doing, but we can certainly allow it. However, if the behavior is harmful to you or someone else, action is necessary and appropriate. Sometimes disagreements are intense enough for people to separate for a while, and that's okay, too. If your relationship is built on a foundation of love (a spiritual partnership) then most likely you will sort things through and remain together for the long term.

The Course gives us many opportunities to practice in its Workbook section. I highly recommend doing the Workbook as well as reading the full text of the Course. This will help make the Workbook more meaningful for you. The intimacy that we all want in our relationships comes when we realize our inherent oneness, and can start making choices based upon this idea of oneness rather than separateness, which the Workbook makes us more aware of.

Another way we tend to make the world of form real is to step into the role of over-responsibility. This role is always one where we find ourselves trying to control the outcome of another's thoughts or behavior; that somehow we feel responsible for their choices, and now it is our job to correct it. Our only job here would be to change our own mind about it, rather than try to control the outcome. There are rare cases where it would be quite appropriate to step in and take charge, and that would reflect the idea in the Course that says it can be quite appropriate to place limits on someone's ability to miscreate if it's harmful to them or someone else. One example of this would be if you feel someone is going to hurt themselves or others, and out of your love and compassion for them and the situation, you do what you can to stop it. This could take the form of someone who is about to drive a car while drunk, or if you saw someone abusing another, such as a child, spouse, or animal. It could be someone trying to attack you, physically, and so you, naturally, try to defend yourself. In these cases, under the Holy Spirit's guidance, it would be very appropriate to take action. It is only stepping into over-responsibility when you attempt to take on another's problems and make them your own, and therefore allow yourself to be at the effect of their behavior, which is also another way of giving power to another to take away your peace.

Showing acknowledgment and appreciation to your partner on a regular basis is another way of fostering a loving, intimate, and compassionate relationship. You don't have to have a reason to acknowledge and appreciate your partner. Just the fact that you are sharing your life with them can be enough to appreciate. Express your feelings of gratitude, and if there are specific things you do feel grateful for, share them, especially if it encourages an attitude or behavior that you really like to see in your partner. Compliment them on the character traits you like, and notice when they are thinking right-mindedly. Then, positively reinforce that behavior by showing your appreciation for them in that moment.

As long as we still believe we are a bodies, we will thrive on acknowledgement, but in truth we are already "known" by love itself. That love has not forgotten us. We have forgotten that we are this love, but we are reinforcing that we are love every instant we see others as they are in truth, in their wholeness, and perfection.

THREE PARTS TO THE MIND

It's helpful to review that we are decision-making minds. In the decision-making mind there are three parts: The right part of the mind, which the Course calls the Holy Spirit, and the wrong part of the mind, which can be equated with the ego, or belief in separation. Then, there is the decision-maker that chooses between these two parts. The Holy Spirit is "the Voice for God." This Voice is in everyone's mind. Many people say they have trouble hearing this Voice. This is because the ego's voice is usually the dominant voice in one's mind until it is trained to think differently. Also, are we *wholly* ready to hear only one voice? Often, we think we know what we want, because we think it's best for us, but this can interfere with hearing the Holy Spirit. It's a matter of letting go of the idea that we know what the best outcome would be in any situation, which will allow room for the Holy Spirit to enter.

The Holy Spirit speaks to us through the feelings of excitement, passion, creativity, curiosity, and the positive emotion of love. The emotion of love, which comes from a loving thought, can take the form of forgiveness, kindness, compassion, gentleness and truth. Listening to the right voice leads to true peace, our natural state. You can trust the Holy Spirit to guide you in your personal relationships so that you don't have to worry about what to say or do. It will come naturally as you build this trust.

The voice of the ego makes up the other part of your mind that believes in separation. The ego thrives at the idea of separation, because its survival depends on it. This is why most of us worry so much about bodily survival. It's the ego's way of maintaining its existence by having you believe you are really a body. We think that without the body, we are dead. That couldn't be further from the truth. There is no death, only life; real life in Heaven. Since the ego will do anything to survive, it will also do anything to sabotage relationships. In fact, its whole existence depends on judging, not forgiving. Its version of love is based on conditions, which is *not* the unconditional love of the Holy Spirit. When you notice the ego impressing its influence over you, you can get really good at catching yourself and choosing the right part of your mind instead. This take lots of practice and discipline, but it is doable. Being vigilant *only* for God is the way out of this madness. In these tough situations, I like to remember Jesus's words from the Course: *In joyous welcome is my hand outstretched to every brother who would join with me in reaching past temptation, and who looks with fixed determination toward the light that shines beyond in perfect constancy.*[12] He emphasizes our need to be focused and motivated, remembering the eternal nature of life.

Finally, there is a part of your mind that chooses between the Holy Spirit and the ego. You do have control over which teacher you choose. This is where your power resides. When you are seeing images in your everyday life, you have the power to decide which teacher you are being loyal to. Which one has more value to you? The answer seems easy, but not always easy to practice. This is because we feel good when we are right. We'll be discussing this in the next chapter; whether you want to be happy or right. The answer to that question will determine the kinds of experiences you have in your life and relationships.

We don't understand the power of the mind. If we let our minds wander, it will wander into oblivion until we remember we can choose with whom we are thinking. Thoughts always precede form. With mind training, you can get very good at directing your mind to think *only* with the Holy Spirit, but this takes great willingness and lots of practice. I've been in many situations where I let my mind wander, and it produced tremendous anxiety. It's still a work in progress for me, but at least I'm aware of what is happening. We will all get to the place where the ego's voice ceases to dominate our minds. That's the good news. The outcome of love is certain. This world is like a roller-coaster ride that has its ups and downs, twists and turns, and plenty of surprises along the way. We decided in Spirit that we wanted to have this adventure, each of us working on various themes to explore to assist us in our awakening. If you find yourself having trouble with one particular situation that keeps repeating in your life, it only means it's a theme you are exploring. You can eventually learn to forgive it, and also understand that it can have no power over you unless you give it power.

This understanding is so important when it comes to any relationship you have that pushes your buttons. This seems to happen more with romantic relationships, although there are many forms of relationships where there is conflict to be resolved. You might feel that your relationship is being tested. Successful relationships begin with a strong foundation of non-judgment, freedom and trust. In other words, you go into the relationship already whole so that you don't become dependent on the other person to make you happy or to satisfy your needs. Most of us do the opposite. We don't already feel whole, so we use the other person to get what we think we lack. If you are confident and in an abundant state of mind, you will trust that you will be given *what* you need *when* you need it. You free the other person to be as they are when you don't try to change them. This is tough! Most of us don't enter relationships with this mindset. We learn as we go along, which is fine. If you truly want your relationship to work, you will explore all avenues until you either find one that works or you decide it's not meant to be. Part of this process involves respecting the other person's choices as well, whether it's a lover, business partner, family member, or friend.

It can be challenging to come from your right mind, especially when things seem to be coming at you. When you start to get the idea that it's coming *from* you based on your own interpretations and reactions to events, then you can start to truly make changes in your life. For example, if your partner projects their own unconscious guilt onto you (which can take many different forms) it's not easy to avoid thinking with the ego. The world was set up that way. This is why it's important to exercise the power of your mind to choose *how* you perceive a person or event.

There is a movie called "A Million Ways to Die in the West." I always got a kick out of that title because it makes me think of this world. The title of this world could be, "A Million Ways the Belief in Separation from God Plays Itself Out." It might seem endless, but fortunately there is a happy ending to the story of the world. The Course says, *The world will end in an illusion, as it began. Yet will its ending be an illusion of mercy. The illusion of forgiveness, complete, excluding no one, limitless in gentleness, will cover it, hiding all evil, concealing all sin and ending guilt forever. So ends the world that guilt had made, for now it has no purpose and is gone.*[13]

For review, when Jesus talks about "sin," he isn't saying it's real. Sin is merely the idea of separation, and the separation from God never happened. As a reminder, that is what accepting the Atonement means in the Course. Notice in the above quote that Jesus says the world was a projection of guilt. This idea runs throughout the Course. If there was no guilt, there would be no experience of a world of time and space. This may seem far out to some, but nonetheless it is the truth.

You can use these ideas in all your relationships to help you remember the truth, which is your wholeness and oneness with all beings. This truth is eternal and can't be changed. Many assaults have been placed on the truth, but they can't be "real" assaults because what you are can't really be threatened in any way. This is the true nature of Spirit. You can't see it, but you can certainly experience it. It is unlike anything in this world. You can't see love, but you can see love in action through one who forgives, who is kind, and who is non-judgmental.

As a reminder, when you find yourself going through a difficult time in your relationship, the idea is to practice coming from your right mind so that you can continue to be inspired as to what actions to take, if any. When your partner says or does something that upsets you, notice your feelings and then practice looking at them with Jesus or the Holy Spirit. This is what it means to look from *Above the Battleground*.[14] You are noticing what is coming up, but without judging yourself or the other person. The ego-based feelings we have are a result of wrong-minded thinking, rather than facts. I'm speaking here of what we would call negative feelings. As mentioned before, the thoughts come first, and the experience follows. This will help you in all your trials, but be kind to yourself if you can't change your mind in the moment. Usually it's a step-by-step process that takes a lot of practice.

The trick of the ego is that it wants you to react to others with upset so that you see the guilt in them, including your partner. You don't have to settle for this interpretation. Let's remember this together and *Be glad you have escaped the mockery of salvation the ego offered you, and look not back with longing on the travesty it made of your relationships. Now no one need suffer, for you have come too far to yield to the illusion of the beauty and holiness of guilt.*[15]

As we move forward together along this journey of undoing the ego, we can remember to settle for nothing less than total and complete faith in Spirit being our identity instead of the shabby substitute of the ego. It offers nothing, while our reality offers everything. The ego's version of the story is about getting things in the world, but at another's expense. The more the ego is undone, the less tempting it will be to need things in the world to make you happy. You will learn what is truly valuable and worthy of a Son of God.

PAGE FOR PERSONAL NOTES

CHAPTER 10

RIGHT OR HAPPY

Seek not outside yourself. For all your pain comes simply from a futile search for what you want, insisting where it must be found. What if it is not there? Do you prefer that you be right or happy?[1]

A man came through my lane at the grocery store with a jug of wine and a bouquet of roses. But before paying, he set the two items aside and said, "I'll be right back." He ran off, only to return a minute later with a second jug of wine and another bouquet of roses. "Two girlfriends?" I asked. "No," he said. "Just one really angry one."

I have no doubt the scenario above might be a common one for many of us! A little humor, though, goes a long way. We need it. Lots of arguments start with someone in the relationship fighting to be right. How many of us take a moment and think about where we are coming from within before we actually start communicating with the upset individual? Do we truly want to be right or happy? Each answer to that question will result in a completely different experience. As I think in this moment about the idea of deliberately "checking in" with myself before I communicate with anyone, the following word comes to mind: Purpose. What is the purpose of my communication? What do I want to come of it? Anytime we set out to do anything or talk to anyone, or have any kind of decision to make, these are the questions we can ask ourselves. Asking these questions encourages more clarity with our goal and sets the stage for a better outcome. We might also be less inclined to get angry when our partner does or says something that normally would hurt us, because we already established the goal at the beginning; that we want to be happy. This is just another way for you to take charge of your mind and not let the ego part of your mind control you.

As I mentioned before, there is a part of the Course worthy of reviewing, and that is the section on *Rules for Decision*. The first couple of steps say that at the beginning of your day say: *Today I will make no decisions by myself.*[2] Then, ask yourself what kind of day you want to have. What kinds of things do you want to experience? What do you want to feel? Then say: *If I make no decisions by myself, this is the day that will be given me.*[3] There are more steps that explain the process when you get off track throughout the day, and I highly recommend reading that part, too. If you are someone reading this book, and haven't read A Course in Miracles, or haven't heard about it before reading this book, I imagine by now you might be thinking various things! Whatever you are thinking, you are right, meaning that it is right for you at this time to be thinking whatever thoughts you are thinking. I've always been an advocate of keeping an open mind, even if certain ideas seem foreign to me. Upon my first reading of the Course, I felt the truth behind the words. The wisdom seemed not of this world. I've never read a document that was as consistent and uncompromising as the Course. It's brilliant. After all, what else would you expect coming from the Holy Spirit?

The Course also emphasizes the value in choosing joy instead of pain. When we insist on being right we are saying the other person is wrong. From the Course's perspective, you are both right because you are a Son of God, and how can a Son of God be wrong? In the world, this plays out quite differently. In partnership, one thing to keep in mind when you find yourself in the heat of an argument is that you probably wouldn't be arguing if either you or your partner decided to be happy instead of right. **It only takes one person to make the decision to be happy to change the quality of your experience in that moment.** I have seen countless situations where two people were "at each other's throats," because each was trying to make the other one wrong, getting absolutely nowhere in their communication. This is because neither one is truly listening to the other. It's an art to listen to your partner with your "third" ear. It can be learned. I am not perfect at this either, but because of practicing the Course, and my training in Psychology, I'm aware of how important it is for people to feel heard. That is the key. When your partner feels heard without judgment, communication will flow.

I've found that when I noticed I was trying to argue that I was right, it didn't really change anything, and I ended up feeling worse as a result. There is a difference when you are trying to correct someone out of a genuine desire to be polite, or making sure they have accurate information, if it involves something important. Another example would be if someone was saying something unloving about you that wasn't true. It would be very appropriate to correct them, so there is no misunderstanding. That can be a very loving thing to do for oneself. Of course, the other person can still choose to hold their perception of you in place, and you can't control what another chooses to believe. If that bothers you, then it's a forgiveness opportunity. The work here would be to do your best to stop making it real for yourself by trying to change the person's mind about you. Just demonstrate love by living it, through forgiving. Sometimes we just need to know when to give it to Spirit, and let it go.

When you are trying to prove you are right (which always serves the ego), then it usually leads to trouble. You may want to question why it is important for you to be right. When we are constantly trying to be right, we apparently feel that our salvation lies in being right rather than happy. In most of my relationships, I frequently catch myself when I notice I am trying to be right. When I stop doing that, and just let the other person be right, there is nothing to bicker about. Bickering usually leads to a full-blown argument. When you give up the need to be right, it is actually a way of joining with the other person, and reinforcing your shared interests. The other way just promotes the idea that you have separate interests and keeps the whole game of separation going. Ask yourself, do you think it would be helpful to state your position, as in the case of helping someone remember a correct appointment time. You will be able to tell the difference by how you feel when you are sharing information. This isn't about being passive, letting someone walk all over you, but just notice where you are coming from inside when you are communicating.

THE ART OF LISTENING

Part of learning to communicate effectively with your partner and to establish intimacy is to practice listening on all levels, not just hearing the words. As I said above, listening is an art. If you understood the underlying meaning of what your partner is trying to say, the need to be right would dissolve. Here are some tips to practice listening to your partner on a deeper level, rather than just hearing the words:

1. **Aside from hearing the words, listen to the deeper meaning behind the words of what your partner is trying to communicate to you.** For example, if one says, *"We don't spend as much time together as we used to."* The underlying meaning may be, *"I am lonely. Somehow I've lost that connection with you, and I want to feel connected again. I am scared."* If we go to the root of this feeling, it is that we have allowed ourselves to disconnect from our Source (the only problem), and the ego was

projecting onto the other person to serve its purpose of main-taining the separation so it could remain "alive" or be validated.

2. **Listen to the tone of voice of your partner as they are speaking to you. They may be saying one thing, but their tone displays the opposite.** For example, one might say, *"I'm doing just great, and things are going so well."* Although they are saying the words, their tone may sound defeated or have a melancholy feel to it. In this case, the words are putting a mask over how they really feel.

3. **Reflect back to your partner what you think they are saying so that they know that you are truly listening and wanting to hear them with accuracy.** It is very easy to twist around someone's words to serve your ego, which is a very sneaky thing the ego does if you don't watch out for it. This example ensures you won't do that. If you don't understand something they've said, ask for clarification. This will really help to show your partner that you care about what they have to say.

4. **Listen to the content of what your partner is saying, aside from just the words themselves.** Do you understand the content? If not, ask for clarification. You might just learn something! As the Course says, *... words are but symbols of symbols. They are thus twice removed from reality.*[4] The content of what they are saying is the important thing, not the specific words they choose. Let's take an example using the Course: Some people do not accept that Jesus is the Voice of the Course, and they dislike the use of Christian terminology. What is important here is the content. What is the message saying? Is it helpful? It's not the words that matter. If you wish, you can substitute other words in your mind that feel better. Just

be aware that if something disturbs you, that's your sign that something needs to be forgiven.

If you practice listening at these different levels, you will not only be a better receiver of information, but a better communicator, because you will be able to respond with a much broader understanding of what you are talking about in the first place. The game of telephone that many of us know so well, where the original message gets distorted as it's passed down from person to person, can take place with just two people when one doesn't get clarification at the beginning of what the conversation is all about. When the message gets twisted in the heat of an argument, and neither one in the relationship makes an effort to truly listen and understand the conversation, it can produce a messy and even violent situation.

Remember in an earlier chapter when I mentioned the TV Comedy show, "Three's Company," with John Ritter? Again, that show was the perfect example of how messages can get distorted, but it was done in a very humorous way. The characters in the show were brilliant at message distortion! I liked how it always came back to love and forgiveness in the end, once everyone understood the misunderstanding. I brought this up again, because it's worthy of watching if you can find the repeats on TV. This actually brings up a great point and reminder about remembering to laugh, even in the most extreme circumstance. We can choose to see the silliness of a situation and remember to laugh. I read a book by Edgar Cayce on healing, and when he was talking about laughter being a healing tool, he said, "Laugh in the most extreme circumstance." Obviously, he didn't mean laughing at another's expense, just remember to laugh. Be light. It's medicine for the soul.

SIGNS YOU ARE MAKING PROGRESS

Would you rather be right or happy? When we marinate in our egos, we are essentially saying we would rather be right. When we give up the need to be right, we are allowing room for happiness to be our state of mind. In the practice of the Course, there are several ways that might help you to see that you are making progress:

1.   The need to be right will be replaced by a desire for happiness and a peaceful mind. This will be so important to you that you will want it above all else. The idea is to create a win-win situation, where everyone benefits.

2.   You will be aware when you are judging, and let it go. When you let go of judgment, you can be a neutral observer. In this position you may find yourself thinking of things as interesting, but not necessarily attached to any particular outcome. You may have a preference, which is natural, but without attachment to results. You will be in a *miracle state of mind*, and this is a very liberating way to live.

3.   You will notice that the things that used to push your buttons aren't having the same effect on you. You will not react with the ego, but respond with love.

4.   You will make decisions without guilt. When there is no guilt, there is clarity. You are sure of what you want, and certain of which way you go.

5.   You will be more aware of when you are confusing love with sacrifice, understanding that love is just itself. Love doesn't require anything or having to do anything. It is a constant, never shifting or changing, regardless of the circumstances. Your direction is freedom, and God is your goal.

The above tips will help you to know if you are on a right-minded track. Remember, we all make mistakes that have to do with our mistaken thinking, and mistakes just call for correction, not punishment. It's about undoing our errors in thinking with the ego as our teacher. When you realize you've chosen the ego, even if you realize it after an argument, the correction can still be made in the mind by choosing again. All of time, which includes the past, present, and future, occurs simultaneously. All of the illusory lifetimes you've ever lived are occurring right now. This is why when you forgive *now*, your forgiveness has an effect on all your other lifetimes. **When one heals, we *all* heal.**

I realize that forgiveness is not always easy, but to repeat an important point, that is because there is still the temptation to perceive forgiveness through the lens of separation instead of oneness. When you start to forgive with the idea of oneness in mind, you understand that the benefits of forgiveness are really for *you*. There is not really another person out there, only a projection of a person. We are projecting this entire dream of time and space, but we forgot that we are projecting, so we make our projections real by reacting to the figures in our dream/projection.

One of the ways out of this mess is to meet attack with love. When you do this, it cancels out the attack so it doesn't grow into something bigger. It remains neutral. It also demonstrates to the one doing the attacking that nothing has happened to change the peace of God within you, and the separation has not occurred. The Son of God is still as God created Him. We are all the Son of God as one. This is what Jesus taught well. He demonstrated that the forgiving of sins wasn't limited to the Priesthood. Anyone could forgive sins because we are all equals. He is teaching us today through the Course what he was teaching then. What a gift this is to us all. Accept the blessing of this gift, and you will be free; free of the fear that can take many forms. There is nothing you have to do, but if you have a choice, why not choose to live the happy dream of forgiveness?

What does it really mean to be right? To be right is to make another wrong. On the level of form, one could certainly make an argument that they are right. But what does that have to do with the big picture? Even if you are right, being right does not undo the ego. It keeps you stuck in it. **If being right might save someone's life, or is**

truly helpful in the sense that it is coming from an inspired place of encouragement rather than to serve the ego, then that can be very loving. It takes practice to trust that your choices are inspired by the Holy Spirit. Again, you will know by how you feel. Feelings and emotions can tell us a lot about our state of mind. In that sense, they are very useful and can be used as a tool to help us get back into alignment with our Source.

In relationships, sometimes you have to have the willingness to compromise. Gary often tells a story about his grandparents. He says, "My grandparents were married for 67 years, until my grandfather passed away. He lived to be 85 and my grandmother lived to be 93. Near the end of his life I asked my grandfather, 'How can you be married for so long? How can you get along with each other for such a long time?' Having a great sense of humor, my grandfather smiled, looked at me and said, 'It's simple. We agreed when we got married that she would make all of the little decisions, and I would make all of the big decisions. And thank God, in the last 67 years there have been no big decisions.'"

Despite his joke, Gary's point was that his grandfather was secure enough in his relationship to not have to be right, but it didn't mean that he didn't assert himself if he thought it was important. **Practicing forgiveness doesn't mean that you let people walk all over you. It means that you watch your reactions so that you don't have to be a victim of outside circumstances. Real power is being at cause and not effect. Being at cause means that you understand that the world you see is an outside picture of an inward condition. This is *your* dream, and it's coming *from* you. If the world is being projected by you, now forgiveness is justified.**

For review, the steps of true forgiveness are that you remember you're dreaming so you don't have to make the dream real. When you understand how the mind works, you can turn the tables on the ego and make the shift to the Holy Spirit. Deep in the mind there is a collective unconscious; only one mind. Your unconscious mind knows that. This is why what you are thinking about other people is really what you believe to be true about yourself. This is an important thought to ponder. Our thoughts do influence us and how we feel. If we are thinking negative thoughts about other people, and those thoughts are coming right back to us, it creates a state of depression. This is also true with the thoughts we think about ourselves. The more we pay attention to whom we are thinking with, the ego or Holy Spirit, the more we start to gain control over our thoughts. Sometimes we need extra help or assistance in changing our minds. There is no shame in this. For example, therapy can be a very helpful tool to assist one in bringing unresolved material to the surface, so it can be forgiven. This doesn't mean we have to overanalyze everything. It only means there may be unexpressed emotions that need to come up for release. The Course talks about healing as being the release from fear. Therapy can be helpful with this. You can always practice forgiveness at the same time. Many couples go to therapy together as a way of expressing their commitment to be supportive of one another and to help their relationship move forward, transforming it into a holy relationship.

I have a movie to recommend for couples, but it's funny whether you are in a romantic relationship or not. It's called *Couples Retreat*, starring Vince Vaughn, Jason Bateman, and Jon Favreau, to name a few. The following is a brief summary from IMDB (Internet Movie Data Base): "A comedy centered around four couples who settle into a tropical-island resort for a vacation. While one of the couples is there to work on the marriage, the others fail to realize that participation in the resort's therapy sessions is not optional." As you might imagine, things turn out to be quite entertaining. Gary and I always watch funny movies when we get the chance. It's not only a way of joining, but reminds us that laughter is healing.

Laughter is necessary, because things can get so serious that we lose our sense of Self. There is a very important law of the mind that says,

As you see him you will see yourself. As you treat him you will treat yourself. As you think of him you will think of yourself. Never forget this, for in him you will find yourself or lose yourself. Whenever two Sons of God meet, they are given another chance at salvation.[5] The special relationships we have with our romantic partners are the ones that contain some of our most difficult forgiveness lessons. This was set up for a reason. There are no accidents and nothing happens by chance. You are always with the people you are meant to be with, even if it's for a temporary period of time. You can use these relationships to your advantage by thinking of them as opportunities to practice forgiveness and undo more unconscious guilt. Even though it's important to watch your thoughts, also pay attention to your feelings, since we act out our aggressions based on our feelings. When you remember to laugh, it lessens the intensity of negative emotions.

REVIEWING THE STEPS OF FORGIVENESS

If you start to get upset, the first step of forgiveness is to identify the cause (recognize you are dreaming) and stop reacting with the ego and start thinking with the Holy Spirit. This is what the Course calls the Holy Instant. It's that instant when you switch from your wrong mind to your right mind. This can be the hardest of the three steps of true forgiveness because the ego has its own story that it's been telling you and wants to keep you away from the mind where it knows you can make a different choice.

The Second step involves turning to the Holy Spirit's interpretation and listening to that Voice. The Holy Spirit will remind you it's not real, because what you are experiencing is not true. You can forgive your partner or any circumstance because nothing has happened in reality. The separation from God has not occurred. The Course says, *Forgiveness recognizes what you thought your brother did to you has not occurred. It does not pardon sins and make them real. It sees there was no sin. And in that view are all your sins forgiven. What is sin, except a false idea about God's Son? Forgiveness merely sees its falsity, and therefore lets it go. What then is free to take its place is now the Will of God.*[6]

If you're thinking that the other person really did something to you (which is making the dream real) then your unconscious mind will interpret that to mean *you* really did something and that you're really guilty. This will reinforce the guilt in your unconscious mind. The opposite is also true: If you're thinking that the other person hasn't really done anything, then your unconscious mind will interpret that to mean that you haven't really done anything either, which means that you're both innocent. **In situations involving a great deal of pain and violence, it's not expected that you just shrug it off and pretend you don't feel your feelings. This is about eventually coming to accept a different interpretation about it so that you don't have to suffer.**

The reason none of us have done anything is because we are the dreamers of our dream, not the figures in the dream, and these figures aren't real. The Course asks, *But who reacts to figures in a dream unless he sees them as if they were real? The instant that he sees them as they are they have no more effects on him, because he understands he gave them their effects by causing them and making them seem real.*[7] This comes back to the idea that our minds contain the dominant ideas, wishes and emotions that we choose to think. If we are using our minds to think with the ego, these thoughts get projected out so that the images we see become the cause of our upset, forgetting that it's just a projection of our own thoughts; our secret wishes.

The third step in forgiveness is seeing with spiritual sight. Spiritual sight has nothing to do with the body's eyes. It has to do with the way you think, which is done at the level of the mind. Other terms the Course uses for this are true Vision or Christ Vision. The Course speaks about the Mind being the *activating agent of spirit.*[8] You activate Spirit in your mind by choosing it; seeing the Christ in others. We are all the Christ, one Son of God. Thinking this way is one of the fastest ways to recognize your own Divine nature. True forgiveness is the path to unconditional love. Eventually, you won't need forgiveness because you will no longer condemn another. Love will just be itself. This is the simplicity of the Course. It's simple in principle, but can be difficult in practice because of the complexity of the ego. **When you no longer desire to be something other than God created you, all that will be left is the beauty of what you have always been and will continue to be into eternity.**

It is okay if you choose to stay here (in the world) a while. No one will take that choice away from you, and you will never be judged for that choice. There will come a time, however, when all beings that appear to be here on the earth plane will accept that their time has come to go home to God for good. Their seeming incarnations will come to a close. You will have transcended the world, but let that not be a sign that your work is done. There might be other people that will need your service, and you can be the light that shines the path to God for them in one form or another. If you choose to take this opportunity, it can be a wonderful way to express your oneness with all beings, because to serve your brother is to serve God. When the whole Sonship as one has transcended the world, it will appear to disappear. God's Son is free. He is free now, but forgot, that is all. So, let's give each other the blessing of forgiveness, taking any opportunity that comes to challenge us, and be certain of which way we go. Let our direction be freedom, and God be our goal. *Let it be. Let it be. Whisper words of wisdom, let it be.*[9]

PAGE FOR PERSONAL NOTES

CHAPTER 11

SPECIAL RELATIONSHIPS

The past is gone; seek not to preserve it in the special relationship
that binds you to it, and would teach you salvation is past and so you
must return to the past to find salvation.[1]

HOW DIVORCE CAN INSPIRE GROWTH

This chapter will focus a bit deeper on understanding what the special relationship is all about. Since divorce is one of the most common experiences people go through in the special relationship, I'd like to elaborate on it. Divorce is often perceived as either wrong or negative in some way. What if it is not wrong, but instead an opportunity to grow beyond where you are now?

I was married for seven years before I met Gary. Overall I had a really nice marriage, and my former husband, Steve, and I are still very good friends. Although I was the one to initiate the divorce, there were a few things that I felt contributed to our parting ways. I felt that the direction my spiritual path was taking was not in alignment with his, and because spirituality was very important to me, this was difficult for me. This doesn't mean that in order for a relationship to work, you have to share the same thought system with your partner. I know of many situations where couples don't practice the same thought system and they stay married, and it works out fine. There are always other factors involved and every situation is unique. Please don't be discouraged if your partner doesn't follow the same spiritual thought system. It can still work. In my situation, I felt specific guidance to make a change. It was as if I had a role to fulfill, a path I was meant to take, and I trusted that.

Another sign that I received that it was time to end the marriage was that it seemed as if there was more time spent on my part thinking about living the single life again, and being attracted to other men. This was happening quite frequently, and I didn't really want to look at it, because the thought of separating from Steve frightened me. Yet, I felt a yearning, and a calling to trust my guidance, which was undeniable. It seemed as if everything was pointing towards this outcome, whether I wanted to face it or not. I loved Steve, but I was growing in ways that weren't compatible with his interests. It created some friction between us to the point where it seemed there was more friction than feelings of joy. This is no one's fault, just the nature of special relationships. I also felt, intuitively, that something was coming that would change the course of my life, and at the time I didn't know what it was, but it was very present within me. I was experiencing these feelings before I met Gary, and I had no idea what was about to happen, or that we would be meeting soon. I thought that I was going to live the single life, and in fact wanted to be single. It's easy to say you will never get married again until, of course, that thing happens that we call "falling in love." I knew that Gary came into my life for a reason, and although I didn't know all the details yet, I felt that we would be sharing a lot together and that it was important that we met. This was reassuring at a time when I felt confused about where my life was going.

My former husband, Steve, is a very caring and loving man, and I can't express enough how grateful I am that we have remained friends. He didn't have to choose to remain friends, and it could have ended up very differently. In my opinion, this showed a level of maturity in him, an open-mindedness, and a willingness to see things differently, even if he wasn't the one that chose to initiate the divorce. I'm not saying we didn't go through our share of sadness, of upset, and the "normal" feelings that go along with getting divorced. Yet, I do believe that our underlying respect for one another made the process easier.

We didn't have children, or own any property, so that made things less complicated. We shared a wonderful dog together named Cozzie, and since Cozzie was very bonded to Steve, it was assumed he would take Cozzie in the divorce. I did have visiting rights! Steve let me come over whenever I wished to see Cozzie, and I am forever grateful for that. Cozzie passed away in 2011, and all I ever wanted was to be able to be there when he passed away and not miss a chance to say good-bye. The last six months or so of Cozzie's life, he wasn't doing very well, and had trouble breathing. His heart was fragile and he needed to be on medication. I went to visit him as often as I could. One day I came over to see him and I looked into his eyes. He was very calm that day and just wanted to lie down. I had a moment with him. Then, early the next morning, Steve called me and said he was taking Cozzie to the emergency room. It was time.

Knowing how often Gary and I were on the road traveling, I couldn't help but notice the blessing of my being home at that time of his passing, so I could say good-bye to my beloved animal companion. He had brought me so much joy and unconditional love for so many years. Steve and I were in the room with Cozzie as he was making his transition. I was talking to him and inviting the Holy Spirit to embrace him in the light and take him where he needed to go. Needless to say, it was difficult, but there was a peace that came over me that he would be free. Later that morning, I saw a light under my door, as if the floor was lit up from underneath the door. I knew it was Cozzie giving me a sign that he was okay. I later dreamed of him playing, with a bright light all around him. He was so happy and so playful, just as he used to be when he was at his peak. We are one forever. You can never lose anyone.

Speaking of animals, my relationships with them are very meaningful. We can learn a lot from them and grow in ways we wouldn't have expected. We have special relationships here on earth, beings in both human and animal form, and those whom we spend more time with than others, but as long as our love doesn't exclude others, that is what is important. Animals teach us that lesson very well. Please pause for a moment and think right now of the ways you observe animals teaching this lesson. God bless them.

For me, personally, what helped me to move through my divorce with some peace was having the consistent thought system of the Course that I could practice daily, and apply to my more difficult moments. I can't stress enough how important it is to have a thought system that works for you that you can focus on. There is no one way that works for everyone, but if you find one that works for you, I encourage you to use it. It keeps the mind focused on your goals so you can bypass some of the endless chatter of the conscious mind. Even if you don't believe in God, it is good to have faith in something.

In my experience, the more I practiced forgiveness the stronger I became, and I was peeling away more and more layers of unconscious guilt. Peace became the dominant thought in my mind more frequently. I wanted it above all else. I made that decision, and now I live up to it to the best of my ability. Even if I'm not always perfect at forgiveness, I know it is the means to achieve the goal of the Course. If I keep my eye on the goal, I will get there. *Those who are certain of the outcome can afford to wait, and wait without anxiety. Patience is natural to the teacher of God. All he sees is certain outcome, at a time perhaps unknown to him as yet, but not in doubt.*[2] I feel gratitude to my former husband, Steve, and to my current husband, Gary, for all the experiences I've had on my path home to God. Having them both in my life and the experiences we've shared, both ups and downs or good and bad, has made me stronger in Spirit, and more vigilant that God is my goal. I bless them both.

SPECIAL LOVE AND SPECIAL HATE

"Special" in this chapter refers to the special relationships we have in the world as opposed to the all-encompassing love of God. In order to understand what special relationships are, it is helpful to understand that the body is the home of specialness. To be special is to be separate, alone, and guilty. Of course you are not really these things, but to the ego, this is its candy. The moment all of us as one mind chose the separation over our oneness with God, it felt good to feel like we had all the power, and to create on our own. When this idea got projected out as a result of guilt, it took the form of having a special, autonomous self that we call the body/personality. To stop the ego/body/personality from wanting to be special is like trying to stop someone seconds before they reach orgasm; it is that desirable, and most tempting to be special. The Course says that *all* God's Sons are special in the sense that none of us are more worthy than another. We are equal as God's one Son.

In the world, we appear to single out an individual or groups of people in the name of love or hate. These are special relationships, because they aren't based on unconditional love. These special relationships are substitutes for the love of God, which we threw away the instant we chose the separation. Specialness takes the form of loving some people, but not others. When we say we love certain people while excluding others, it is special love. Obviously, we won't love everyone romantically. The Course is referring to the unconditional love of God. If we single out certain people to hate, it is special hate. This is how the ego makes itself real, by having degrees of love; some people are worthy of love and some are not.

The ego hates anything that reminds itself that it isn't real. The ego, being a vicious thought system, will sometimes see an expression of love as an attack. This is why some people may give you a dirty look when you smile at them, or try to attack you when you are being kind. Forgive them when that happens so you can be a reminder that only love is real and demonstrate that their "attack" had no effect on you. Remember what we said about the ego in chapter one? Its range goes from *suspiciousness to viciousness.* Once this is understood, it will help you to let go of the idea that your ego is your salvation.

When I first read the following paragraph in the Course, I was astounded at how much the ego has tricked us into thinking we understand the nature of love. Our special love relationships (those we choose to spend the most time with) may seem very genuine and have good intentions to the conscious mind, but unconsciously there is dependency, the need for control and the need to fulfill a lack. This is what we hate. Instead of being totally dependent on God as our only Source of strength and supply, we've projected that dependency on our special love relationships. Here is the quote from the Course I am referring to:

> *The special love relationship is an attempt to limit the destructive effects of hate by finding a haven in the storm of guilt. It makes no attempt to rise above the storm, into the sunlight. On the contrary, it emphasizes the guilt outside the haven by attempting to build barricades against it, and keep within them. The special love relationship is not perceived as a value in itself, but as a place of safety from which hatred is split off and kept apart. The special love partner is acceptable only as long as he serves this purpose. Hatred can enter, and indeed is welcome in some aspects of the relationship, but it is still held together by the illusion of love. If the illusion goes, the relationship is broken or becomes unsatisfying on the grounds of disillusionment.[3]*

Basically, the unconditional love the Course is speaking about is found outside time and space, in our reality with God. The passage above is addressing the illusory perceptions we have about love, as well as the idea that special love is really a mask over special hate. This is far from the experience of reality or pure love. Pure love can be expressed in the world on occasion by those who have remembered God and His perfect love. Jesus is an example of one who remembered God and His true nature. This is why he could be friends with tax collectors, prostitutes, lepers, and people to be feared, deemed unworthy, or not to be trusted. *Perfect love casts out fear. If fear exists, then there is not perfect love. But: Only perfect love exists. If there is fear, it produces a state that does not exist. Believe this and you will be free. Only God can establish this solution, and this faith **is** His gift.*[4]

Remember, none of us came into the world to be perfect in regards to behavior. We have all misunderstood our true nature, because we forgot about it when we appeared to be born into a body. Everyone is in the same boat here. **The purpose of looking at our special relationships is not to feel guilty, but to transform them into holy relationships, which is the focus of this book. The Holy Spirit would never take away our special relationships, because He knows they are great learning aids.**

We are born into special relationships, those that start with our families, and that expand to what becomes our "inner" circle, those we spend the most time with, such as our friends, co-workers, and acquaintances. In special relationships, we have some sort of investment in someone, and when things don't go the way we think they should, we feel we've lost. That is because we've become attached to an outcome; an outcome that we assigned to the other person. When he or she doesn't fulfill our wishes, something has gone wrong. Special relationships are based on dependency, not real love, until we learn to remove the blocks to the awareness of love's presence, which we can do through forgiveness.

Special relationships can take many forms, including our attachments to substances, situations, places, and things. We think our salvation lies in them, and this can lead to abuse of any kind. In these situations, what leads to the abusive thinking or behavior is letting the ego be our teacher, believing indeed that our salvation lies in this special form. What we need to do in these situations is change our teacher to the Holy Spirit, who would help us change our minds about it and think differently, letting go of our attachment that this form is what will save us. If a certain symbol is helping you to move forward without fear, and you are not abusing it, then it can be a helpful tool for a while. The key is having a deeper understanding of what is happening, and why, so that you can eventually forgive the situation. Even if you still use the symbol in some way, you can do it knowing why you are doing it. You can still practice the uncompromising message of the Course. Someone who may appear to have great limitations or be compromised in some way might be making tremendous progress on their spiritual path. Also, just the opposite can happen. Someone who one might judge as having it all together, and having the perfect life from the outside, could be delaying their progress for reasons we can't see. The point is that none of us can judge accurately what other people need for their spiritual growth.

At the highest level, we all chose the lives we were born into for a reason. There are no accidents. This can be applied to our relationships as well as to the people we meet during the course of our lives. The Course says, *There are no accidents in salvation. Those who are to meet will meet, because together they have the potential for a holy relationship. They are ready for each other.*[5] This means, even the relationships where we have the most trouble forgiving, are there for a reason. If we had everything figured out and expressed perfect love all the time, we wouldn't need to have the experience of incarnation. We are learning through our special relationships that we are not guilty, and are worthy of experiencing a life of joy.

All of us will have special relationships while we appear to be here, but the Holy Spirit has a different purpose for using them, apart from the ego's purpose. The Holy Spirit uses these relationships to teach His lessons of love. Real love is changeless, eternal, and unconditional, so it doesn't exclude anyone or anything. This doesn't mean that the form of your relationships will always be the same, only that you will love everyone equally regardless of the form of the relationship. Of course we cannot, nor would we want to, be romantic with everyone we meet, but we can love people because we were created the same and are exactly the same as God. The way we treat other people is an indicator of how we feel about ourselves.

For a review, in the world of relationships, we have special love and special hate. Those whom we think we love are special love relationships, while those we think we hate are special hate relationships. In other words, we single out people and say we love some and hate others. If we think in terms of oneness and wholeness, it would have to mean that whenever we love another, we love ourselves. Whenever we hate another, we hate ourselves. Any thought you have that goes out to another is really about *you*. This is why it is important to pay attention to your thoughts. You are defining yourself every moment by how you think about other people.

There is really only one special relationship, and that is with the ego. We decided that we wanted to be special and different the instant we chose the separation over God's love. Jesus makes it very clear in the Course that you alone are not special. He is speaking to the egos we believe we are. We believe we are different than everybody else, have "gifts" that others don't have, and we feel grateful that we are abundant when we see others suffering. This is because we think we know what a real gift is and that we understand what it means to feel gratitude.

To feel gratitude for having so much because you see other's suffering is not real gratitude, but separation. A very common saying is that we should be grateful for having food on our plates, clothes on our backs, and roofs over our heads, because look at all those who are suffering and have no such things! Jesus makes a reference to this in the Course. He says, *Gratitude is a lesson hard to learn for those who look upon the world amiss. The most that they can do is see themselves as better off than others. And they try to be content because another seems to suffer more than they. How pitiful and deprecating are such thoughts! For who has cause for thanks while others have less cause? And who could suffer less because he sees another suffer more?*[6]

This type of gratitude is found in the special relationship. Many are well-intentioned, but real gratitude comes from being grateful that God has blessed us all equally with His gifts of unconditional love, peace, and joy, and that we remain exactly as He created us, as His one Son. **We are all headed in the same direction of freedom, with God as our goal**.

Once you come to understand the function of special relationships, you can then transform them to reflect the Holy Spirit's love instead of the ego's hate. Again, every relationship is a lesson in love. We are learning that love is changeless, and that no matter how difficult a relationship might be, you are with the exact person you are meant to be with so that you can learn the lessons you came here to learn. You can be joyful and peaceful regardless of the circumstances, using every challenge as an opportunity to choose love over fear.

In some cases, as we discussed in an earlier chapter, you might be guided to leave a relationship or the form of it may change. In other relationships, you might find it impossible to leave, not understanding the reason. This might mean that there is still something your soul wants to learn, and there is work to be done. There is some kind of holy experience you are working towards, and the opportunity is right there in front of your face to bring healing to it. These are never easy relationships, but they hold potential for tremendous growth if you allow yourself to move through them, trusting you are never alone. Also, Spirit might be preparing you to help others in their growth as well. Having been through some difficult times, you might have more empathy for others.

EXERCISE IN FURTHERING YOUR
FORGIVENESS PRACTICE

Think of someone right now who you don't like for whatever reason or you may love, but feel resentment towards. Whoever popped in your mind first is probably the one to use for this exercise. Visualize this person's face in your mind. As you are seeing this person in your mind, can you think of them with love and innocence; without judgment? Can you see them from a neutral place without a feeling of intensity or agitation? If you can, you are seeing with the Holy Spirit. If not, there is something unforgiven that needs to come to the surface, observed, then forgiven. Do a forgiveness thought process that you like, and do your best to mean it, rather than just saying the words. Think about what you are saying, knowing that what you think about another, you also think about yourself. Try and see this person offering you a blessing, which you can receive and then offer one in return. Without this person triggering you, you wouldn't know there is unconscious guilt in your mind needing to be undone. What an opportunity and potential gift for healing!

You can do this very short exercise with anyone. Remember, just because you are forgiving people (which is really forgiving yourself), it doesn't mean you have to hang around with them. You don't have to agree with what they say or do. Forgiveness is for the benefit of your mind, so that you can be released from being a prisoner of your own thinking. As you probably know by now, this takes work. This is the real work of our lives. It's not our jobs we go to everyday to make money for ourselves and our retirement that is the most important thing. What is important is that we are using our lives and our relationships in service to growth and understanding of who we are. Are we being of service to others, being kind, compassionate and forgiving?

Whenever you give your relationship over to the Holy Spirit for healing, it becomes a gift you are giving to Him. Whenever you feel fear in your relationship, and if you don't know what to do or say, Jesus asks us not to ask him to remove the fear, or even what it is we should say. Instead he is encouraging us to ask him for help in seeing other people as sinless. Fear is caused by a lack of trust and faith that we are still at home with a loving God. The ego has us believe He is a punishing God. So, we need to practice seeing ourselves and others *without* sin, which means we recognize that God is love, and therefore can claim it for ourselves. When you are sure that the outcome of love is certain, which means going high enough in your thinking (seeing with true perception), there will be no fear.

In the context of romantic relationships, I can't imagine a better aphrodisiac than to be fearless. True intimacy is the outcome of raw, clear communication, where the foundation is love, non-judgment, freedom, and joy. Most people just get along as best they can in their relationships, but there is so much more that can be yours if you allow it in. This also requires doing the work necessary to undo the guilt in your own mind, so you can enjoy to the fullest the benefits of a shared union with your partner.

I frequently watch how people respond to each other in their relationships. I love sitting at a restaurant or coffee shop, just watching people interact. I think that comes from my interest in Psychology. There has always been a part of me that is fascinated by people's reactions to events and people around them. Although I never intervene, I often find myself thinking what I would say to them if given the opportunity. Most people haven't been taught about the mind and the proper use of its power. It's mainly about changing your thinking patterns. Most people don't know that they are choosing their thoughts, positive or negative, which determine the types of experiences they have. After all, most of us were not taught that we are decision-making minds, but instead believe that we are at the effect of people and the world. We just automatically do what people tell us to do, or follow the collective consciousness of the world at large, not really thinking for ourselves.

Fortunately, more people are waking up to the fact that they have the power to think for themselves.

I'd like to highlight a couple of paragraphs from the Course on special relationships and then comment on them. It is my intention that this will help you to gain clarity on the purpose of the special relationship, so that you can make the shift to a holy relationship with more awareness. This is what the Course says:

> You cannot love parts of reality and understand what love means. If you would love unlike to God, Who knows no special love, how can you understand it? To believe that **special** relationships, with **special** love, can offer you salvation is the belief that separation is salvation. For it is the complete equality of the Atonement in which salvation lies. How can you decide that special aspects of the Sonship can give you more than others? The past has taught you this. Yet the holy instant teaches you it is not so.[7]

> Because of guilt, all special relationships have elements of fear in them. This is why they shift and change so frequently. They are not based on changeless love alone. And love, where fear has entered, cannot be depended on because it is not perfect. In His function as Interpreter of what you made, the Holy Spirit uses special relationships, which you have chosen to support the ego, as learning experiences that point to truth. Under His teaching, every relationship becomes a lesson in love.[8]

The meaning behind these statements is that our love has to be total in order to be true love. As I pointed out earlier, this doesn't mean we will go around romantically loving everyone in the same way. It only means that we aren't excluding our love in general from any part of the Sonship. Loving the whole Sonship equally means you are loving yourself. When we come back to the idea that there is only one mind appearing as 7-8 billion people, then we will understand that we, essentially, *are* those 7-8 billion people! The ultimate illusion is that we don't come from the same source. It's a trick of the ego mind to have us believe that we are different from each other. In form, we will look and behave differently. In content, we are the same and come from the same source. This can be a hard pill to swallow if there is someone that you despise in your life, or even someone you don't know. It could be a political figure or anyone you see on television that you can't stand. You might have negative thoughts about the person and start to get all worked up when you see them come on the screen. What is happening here is that the unconscious guilt in your mind is coming to the surface, being projected outside yourself so that you see the guilt in another person instead of where it really is; in your mind. If there were no guilt in your mind, you wouldn't be upset.

What I've described above can be applied to your personal relationships. Once you know that there is only one of us appearing to be here, then you can ask yourself the following question when you see someone doing something you don't like: *Would I condemn myself for doing this?*[9] If you find yourself saying "Yes" to this question, another question to ask is "Why would I condemn myself?" When you free another from all the negative thoughts you were holding about them, you are preparing yourself for your own freedom. If you practice forgiveness instead of judging, and you are doing this with authenticity, the Course says that *you will begin to sense a lifting up, a lightening of weight across your chest, a deep and certain feeling of relief. The time remaining should be given to experiencing the escape from all the heavy chains you sought to lay upon your brother, but were laid upon yourself.*[10]

You might want to try practicing this exercise with your partner or anyone you feel is causing you pain. As a reminder, even though this book is focused mainly on romantic relationships, most of the content can be applied to any relationship you are having with someone or something. It's the content that matters, and what you choose to do with it. This is also true for anything that you read. Look for the quality of the message, not so much the form in which it is given. Does the information inspire you? Does it help you to be more peaceful? Does it make you think? Does it give you another interpretation to consider, whether you agree with it or not? Are you allowing open-mindedness to enter, even if it goes against your belief system?

HONORING HELEN SCHUCMAN AND THE SCRIBING OF A COURSE IN MIRACLES

Since this book is about relationships, it's often noted that Helen had a complicated relationship with Bill Thetford, her colleague and co-scribe of the Course. However, what they accomplished together is a testament to their willingness to find a better way of relating, which inspired the Course to come through. To honor both of them, but also give you some background on their relationship, the following passage is posted on the website of *The Foundation for Inner Peace* (the original publisher of A Course in Miracles):

"Helen Schucman and Bill Thetford were an unlikely team in scribing A Course in Miracles. As career-oriented psychologists working closely together at the Columbia-Presbyterian Medical Center, they were attempting to develop and strengthen the Center's Psychology Department. While their professional interests and goals for the department were compatible with each other, their personalities certainly were not. Helen's overtly critical and judgmental stance was juxtaposed with Bill's quiet and more passively aggressive personality, and they clashed constantly.

It was therefore a rather startling event when, in the Spring of 1965, Bill delivered an impassioned speech to Helen in which he said that he was fed up with the competition, aggression, and anger which permeated their professional lives, extended into their attitudes and relationships, and pervaded the department. He concluded and told her that "there must be another way" of living—in harmony rather than discord—and that he was determined to find it. Equally startling, and to their mutual surprise, Helen agreed with Bill and enthusiastically volunteered to join him in a collaborative search to find this other and better way.

It was as if Helen had waited all her life for this particular moment, which triggered a series of internal experiences for her that carried through the summer. These included heightened dream imagery, psychic episodes, visions, and an experience of an inner voice. The experiences also became increasingly religious, with the figure of Jesus appearing more and more frequently to her in both visual and auditory expressions.

This period of preparation culminated on the evening of October 21, 1965, when the now familiar voice of Jesus said to Helen: "This is a course in miracles, please take notes." Troubled, she called Bill immediately, and he reassured her that she was not going mad. He suggested she write down what was being dictated to her, and that he would look at it with her early the following morning at the office. Helen did just that, which is how the scribing of A Course in Miracles *began. As Helen later described the experience:*

"The Voice made no sound, but seemed to be giving me a kind of rapid, inner dictation which I took down in a shorthand notebook. The writing was never automatic. It could be interrupted at any time and later picked up again. It made obvious use of my educational background, interests and experience, but that was in matters of style rather than content. Certainly the subject matter itself was the last thing I would have expected to write about."

Helen retired from Columbia-Presbyterian Medical Center in 1977, and died in New York City on February 9, 1981. Bill took early retirement from Columbia University School of Physicians and Surgeons in 1978. He moved then to Tiburon, California where he served as a Consultant Medical Specialist in Family Medicine at Travis Air Force Base and as a Director of The Center for Attitudinal Healing in Tiburon. Dr. Thetford co-edited "Choose Once Again" selections from the Course. He also made recordings of his favorite sections of the Course with Dr. Gerald G. Jampolsky. He relocated to La Jolla, California in 1986 and died on July 4, 1988 on a trip to Tiburon."

Also, you might find it interesting to read the following additional statements about the Course's beginning from Robert Skutch, an American author, and one of the founders of *The Foundation for Inner Peace* (original publisher of A Course in Miracles) along with the late, great Judith Skutch Whitson, Kenneth Wapnick, Helen Schucman, and Bill Thetford:

"Helen Schucman, Ph.D., was a most unlikely person to scribe A Course in Miracles, as was William Thetford, Ph.D., the person to assist her. In reality, in the Psychology Department of Presbyterian Hospital in New York which Dr. Thetford headed and where they both worked, Helen was his assistant. Both also held positions at Columbia University's College of Physicians and Surgeons, where Dr. Thetford was Professor of Medical Psychology, and Dr. Schucman as Associate Professor.

At the time, Helen Schucman not only had considered herself an Atheist, but she also felt that any spiritual-type material – such as eventually appeared in the Course – was "rubbish." William Thetford considered himself a "down-to-earth" pragmatist and psychologist, whose reality was adequately and safely defined through basic, materialistic world views.

However, their professional work environment was wrought with a multitude of problems and tensions. Perhaps, because of this, each especially needed the other's support and sustenance in order to cope with the enormous difficulties they faced. And it eventually became obvious to them that they had to do something to try to change the extant feelings of hostility and resentment that surrounded them."

It was the tension between Helen and Bill, as described above, that inspired them to say: "There has to be a better way." That better way came through Helen as the Voice of Jesus, starting Helen on a journey she would never forget: Writing over 1300 pages of material speaking the Word of God; the main message being that there is only one reality, that of God. Helen knew this was a special assignment, and that is why she continued the writing until it was completed; over seven years-worth of material.

Jesus knew we wouldn't always believe in the ideas He was presenting, and that is why He also gave the Workbook, which contains 365 lessons, one for every day of the year. The first part is helping people undo the way they see now, and the second part helps us with correcting our perceptions. It's very clear that the content of the Course comes from outside time and space. The consistency and uncompromising nature of the message is astounding. This path is not meant for everyone to accept all at once. It is one form of the universal curriculum. All paths lead to God in the end, but the Course goes right to the root cause of the world we see, what to do about it, and how to wake up from the dream. This just gives you a little piece of the backstory of the Course. For a more thorough understanding of how it came about and why, take a look at the book, *Journey Without Distance*, by Robert Skutch. There are more recommended readings about the Course in the back of this book.

Coming back to special relationships, the more the Course is studied and practiced, the more it becomes very clear that our special love relationships are *not* the same thing as the pure, unconditional love of God. As I mentioned, it is quite normal to have special relationships in the world while we appear to be here. They are our classrooms of forgiveness. All it takes is a brief look back at some of the most painful relationships we've ever had, and all of them fall into specialness. We can certainly learn a lot from them, and that is what they are for; not for condemnation, but forgiveness. Next, we'll move into yet another step on our journey forward into transforming our special relationships into holy ones. We will move into the realm of how to have fearless communication with our partners, or at least start moving in that direction; the direction of freedom.

PAGE FOR PERSONAL NOTES

CHAPTER 12

FEARLESS COMMUNICATION

When the body ceases to attract you, and when you place no value on it as a means of getting anything, then there will be no interference in communication and your thoughts will be as free as God's.[1]

A BUDDHIST STORY

A *fierce and terrifying band of samurai was riding through the coun-tryside, bringing fear and harm wherever they went. As they were approaching one particular town, all the monks in the town's monastery fled, except for the abbot. When the band of warriors entered the monastery, they found the abbot sitting at the front of the shrine room in perfect posture. The fierce leader took out his sword and said, "Don't you know who I am? Don't you know that I'm the sort of person who could run you through with my sword without batting an eye?" The Zen master responded, "And I, sir, am the sort of man who could be run through by a sword without batting an eye.*

This story is about letting go of attachment to the body, allowing for clear, unobstructed communication to flow through you. It's not that different than Jesus's response to the crucifixion. When the body is used for the ego's purpose, it becomes a thing of destruction, decay, and death, which will be reflected in your relationships through the dynamic of projection. When it is used to allow the Holy Spirit to communicate Its message of truth, it can only heal and inspire, but not harm. Therefore, when we remove the obstacles to peace in our awareness, we are free to express with love instead of fear.

Our minds are often clogged with fearful thoughts, many of them being about the body. If we don't empty ourselves of these thoughts, it can affect all aspects of our lives, throwing it off balance. In relationships, learning how to take care of the mind will assist you in having healthy and effective communication with your partner, because the body thoughts will fade into the background. Jesus says that when we are not thinking with God, or at least turning our thoughts over to the Holy Spirit, then we are not really thinking at all, which means we're definitely not really communicating in the truest sense of the word. He is saying that if love isn't present, the communication is meaningless. Pure non-dualism says that anything that can shift or change, and doesn't come from love, is not real. It takes a lot of mind training to learn to discern the difference between the two states of mind (love and fear), but it can be done if you are committed to it.

In all relationships, not just romantic ones, one can learn to communicate freely and effectively, without fear. Fearful communication is usually the result of the guilt in the unconscious mind playing itself out. Guilt can play itself out in various ways, one being the idea that we need others' approval for things we say and do. We want to feel validated, justified, and acknowledged. This is a normal way to feel when you are in a body, but if you are constantly seeking the approval of others, you are actually giving your power away and are reinforcing the belief that you cannot think for yourself. It also makes it difficult to trust yourself to make good decisions. This is a crippling of the mind. This happens when we don't have the confidence to honor ourselves and stay true to our path. It has taken me many years to feel even slightly comfortable with expressing my true self and honoring my choices. It has become easier over time, since I started practicing forgiveness.

The fear in the unconscious mind comes from not feeling worthy of being happy, of having nice things, of having our lives go well, and being the magnificent beings that we are. As a result, we choose to punish ourselves by repressing our feelings and self-honoring choices, hoping that someone or something else will fix us and make everything okay. It is this kind of thinking that keeps us stuck being a victim and in fearful communication. Perhaps we were taught at a young age that communicating one's feelings or expressing emotions was a problem. Over time, if that is a belief you continue to hold, it will take lots of practice to learn to communicate with confidence instead of fear. Many of us weren't taught how to express emotions in a safe space. Eventually, those repressed emotions will want to come to the surface and be released.

If you are currently in a relationship where you and your partner are having problems with communication, it can be a helpful tool to go to couples therapy where you can each express what needs to be expressed in a supportive and loving environment. Some of you might have had negative experiences as a child while attempting to communicate something that was important to you, only to be shut down and silenced. Eventually, repressed feelings will come to the surface so that you can release and forgive them if you choose to do so. You can become a powerful communicator and do so without blaming or judging your partner or whoever you are attempting to communicate with.

As I mentioned, guilt can play itself out in many ways. One way is when we don't trust that we have the strength that comes from God to help us communicate effectively and without fear. There is great fear of being judged by another person, being mocked, not being taken seriously or not being understood. These are all very common fears, and these fears can be transformed into love if you allow yourself to step outside the box you have placed yourself in. The physical body is limited, but your mind is unlimited. The body can be used as a communication device to let the Holy Spirit's love flow through you, unimpeded by external factors. Many great channeling masters do this by getting their conscious, chattering mind out of the way so that they can be a clear vessel for higher wisdom to flow through. You can learn this, too, and practice with your partner. They don't even have to know you are practicing with them. It can be a fun game.

HOW TO PRACTICE FEARLESS COMMUNICATION

Let's use an example of how you can move through a fearful situation as you are about to communicate an issue to your partner. The first step is finding an appropriate time to talk to your partner, when he or she agrees to communicate with you, or at the very least, is in a good mood. Ask your partner if it's a good time, and if not, schedule another time when it is more convenient. If there is no commitment on the part of your partner, gently remind yourself that you can trust the process. Then, do the best you can with it. If it is a situation that requires some resolution in order for you to stay in the relationship, as in the case of abuse, addiction, or any other more serious matter, then follow your guidance as to what is most loving and honoring for yourself, which will offer your partner a chance to change his or her ways. It will become clear how important the relationship is to either of you, depending on whether there is movement toward a direction of healing in some form.

There are things you can pay attention to before you start the process of effectively communicating with your partner. Notice if fear is present within you. Be self-aware. If you aren't aware of the fear, you can't transform it into love. Next, clarify your goal. What is the purpose of your discussion? What do you want to come of it? If your purpose is to make yourself right, you may want to reconsider having the discussion. If your purpose is to join with your partner and find common ground, sharing what you feel without judging your partner, you are on the right track. Then, when you decide what you want to come of it, trust you will be given the means to lead you to the best possible solution for the highest good of all concerned. The important thing is to let go of attachment to any particular outcome, so you will not be disappointed if your expectations aren't met. Your partner may not have much to say about what you've shared, or may not want to respond much at all, even though he or she agreed to the discussion. If this upsets you or disturbs your peace in any way, it is a forgiveness opportunity. You can silently apply a forgiveness thought process, remembering that no one has the power to take away your peace, unless you give them that power. As you are speaking to your partner, if you notice fear, tell yourself (silently) that this will pass, and then think of these lines from the Course: *The guiltless mind cannot suffer.*[2] *I am as God created me. His Son can suffer nothing. And I am His Son.*[3]

When you ask the questions above in your mind and get clarity upfront on the purpose of your discussion, it will lessen fear because you will feel more confident with your intention. You might want to remind yourself that God is not fear, but love. Practice being mindful of being as open and honest as you can, without projecting onto your partner and making them wrong. Be kind. Kindness goes a long way. The key is to always forgive yourself if you feel fear in any form. When fear is present, it is a sure sign that you are trusting in your own strength. Turn it over to the Holy Spirit. Usually, when we fear something, we are confusing symbol with Source. We think we are fearful because of something outside of us, when the source of the fear is always a choice made in the mind. If it is in the mind, you can change your mind about it. You do have that power. You don't have to be a victim of fear. Bringing the fear back to the cause in the mind will help you feel more powerful, because you can actually do something about it. Even if fear is still present, you don't have to suffer. That is also a choice. For example, I still experience some anxiety, but I do my best to not let it take away the peace of God within me, and ruin my day. I just accept it and do the best I can to take care of myself, doing what feels loving and comforting.

Comparing ourselves with others also leads to fear, when we believe that someone else has something that we lack. Comparison is an ego device. We often confuse form with content. In form (the physical world) there will always be things that others appear to have that we don't, but it is not the form that matters. It is the content that matters, and in content we all have equal opportunity to choose which teacher in our minds we are being loyal to. Comparing ourselves to others comes from lack, and it is a waste of time, because we are in no position to judge what is best for anyone, including ourselves, nor can we even judge accurately. This is when we want to call upon the Holy Spirit for help. Remember this from the Course, once again: *It is necessary for the teacher of God to realize, not that he should not judge, but that he cannot. In giving up judgment, he is merely giving up what he did not have. He gives up an illusion; or better, he has an illusion of giving up. He has actually merely become more honest. Recognizing that judgment was always impossible for him, he no longer attempts it. This is no sacrifice. On the contrary, he puts himself in a position where judgment **through** him rather than **by** him can occur.*[4]

The following will help you move through fear: When you turn your judgments over to the Holy Spirit for Him to reinterpret for you, then whatever you say or do will be loving. Words don't matter as much as the essence behind the words you say. The ego will always try and resist the idea that you can be peaceful and not affected by what happens, and it even makes you feel guilty for not reacting with concern. It's not that you don't respond, rather are you coming from fear or love? **If there is turbulence around you, your thoughts do not have to be turbulent. If there is violence around you, your thoughts do not have to be violent.** The choice is yours to make. The freedom from fear and from fearful communication lies in the awareness of the thoughts you are choosing at any given moment. Now you know you can do something about it; return to your decision-making mind and choose the Holy Spirit as you sort out the situation.

Intervention is for ourselves first, then, perceiving with our right minds, we can naturally extend our love to another person. Following that, whatever we say or do will be helpful. Whenever we feel fearful, love is not present, and it's because we have let our minds wander, not allowing the Holy Spirit to guide us. The cause of fear is in the mind and has nothing to do with outside circumstances, although it seems so. It takes abundant willingness to stay mindful of this, and to practice cultivating healthier habits of thought, so they become rules by which we live. If anger is involved, the Course says, *Anger always involves projection of separation, which must ultimately be accepted as one's own responsibility, rather than being blamed on others. Anger cannot occur unless you believe that you have been attacked, that your attack is justified in return, and that you are in no way responsible for it.*[5] This doesn't mean we won't get angry sometimes. However, it's helpful to know that we can bring peace instead to ourselves at any moment, when we decide to change our minds about what the anger represents.

There is nothing harder than accepting that we made all this up: the world, our special relationships, and the story of our lives. The ego's strategy doesn't have to become the model for your learning when you understand that there is another perception you can hold about the script that's playing out before you. Blame just keeps one stuck, like a tire spinning its wheels when it's stuck in the mud. What gets it unstuck is to remove the mud (our judgments and grievances).

Another tool you can use in communication with your partner, or anyone, is to be completely honest and tell the person that you are feeling fearful. Take responsibility for the fear, and be aware if you are projecting that fear onto the other person as well. When you are coming from honesty and authenticity, it is much more likely that your partner will respond without fear, and might even begin to empathize with you so that true understanding can take the place of the fear.

In the St. Francis Prayer for Peace, it is said, "Grant that I may not so much seek to be understood, than to understand." Just as you do not have to seek for Love, just *be* love; you do not have to seek to be understood, rather seek to understand. When you are truly coming from this place of understanding, there is nothing to seek. It is very easy to say you want these things, but to mean it is to apply it in your everyday life.

I've had to admit to myself on many occasions that I must have wanted something other than truth, and I knew that by how I felt. My emotions were a signal to me, telling me that I must have chosen the ego as my teacher because peace was not in my awareness. Your emotions will tell you what track you are on if you pay attention. What attracts me to the Course is its purely non-dualistic thought system that says: if you believe in God, there are two things that appear to be true, the Kingdom of God, and the world of man, but only one of these is true, the Kingdom of God. I know that if I feel anything other than true peace, I am making the choice for the world of man, with the ego as my teacher. I have to admit that when I am choosing anything other than God, I must be deciding that I don't want *only* God just yet. I do find that I want to experience the choice for God on a much more consistent basis. For me, personally, it is a much happier and peaceful path, and the benefits are worth the effort.

THREE POINTS OF PROGRESS

This leads me to what I call *the three points of progress,* which are three, positive and life-changing shifts that have taken place within me since I started studying and practicing the Course. The shifts that take place when you are on this path are not limited to these three things, which I've touched on in another chapter. Sharing them again may help you to determine where you are on the path as well, and will help you move from fear to love. Here they are with a little more detail:

1. **Things that used to upset you no longer have the same impact as they used to.** With this awareness comes the realization that you are never upset for the reason you think, and that nothing outside of you (person, place, or thing) is the cause of your upset. You also understand that when you get upset at someone or something, you first made it real in your own mind, or else you wouldn't have identified with it in the first place. The real reason that you are upset (and this includes even a mild annoyance) is that you have chosen the ego as your teacher. It is the ego thought system that is upsetting, not the situation itself. Practice not making it real, because it's a dream.

2. **You would rather be happy than right.** With this attitude, you are realizing that being right is just not worth all the energy. How can "winning" bring you joy when another suffers? You start to realize that being happy brings you a much greater benefit. You can be at peace regardless of what is happening. We live in a world of competition where there is always a winner and a loser, and I'm not just talking about sports. When you win at someone else's expense, then you've both lost; just as when you need to be right, which makes the other person wrong, then you are both wrong. This is because neither party is seeing with correct perception, but rather through the eyes of judgment. Instead, practice recognizing your shared interests. We have shared interests because we share the same mind. Even though our paths may look different in form, in content they are the same. We are all on a path to awakening.

3. **You are in a miracle state of mind much more often.** With this attitude, you find yourself automatically forgiving instead

of automatically judging. You are now in a state of miracle readiness, always aware of the two thought systems that are available to you, that of the ego or the Holy Spirit, knowing that whatever choice you make is establishing your identity as you believe it to be. Further, a miracle is a shift in perception; it is forgiveness. Practicing forgiveness of the everyday challenges of life will make you much better at automatic forgiveness. If your chosen path is A Course in Miracles, then reading the text of the Course makes the Workbook more meaningful. Also, doing the Workbook exercises makes the *goal* of the Course possible. Memorizing ideas won't do it. Learn to generalize the lessons, making them equally applicable to everyone and everything you see. This is the key.

The three points above, if continuously pondered and practiced, can literally change your life from a life of fear to a life of love. Everything gets better, including your communication with other people, regardless of the type of relationship. Other people do not even need to know you are practicing a unique thought system. That is because there is only one mind, appearing as many different bodies. **When one is forgiven, we are all forgiven. A past hate towards someone can become a present love, reinforcing the holy relationship.**

Here is more wisdom from the Course regarding the holy relationship: *When you feel the holiness of your relationship is threatened by anything, stop instantly and offer the Holy Spirit your willingness, in spite of fear, to let Him exchange this instant for the holy one that you would rather have. He will never fail in this. But forget not that your relationship is one, and so it must be that whatever threatens the peace of one is an equal threat to the other.*[6] This passage describes the process of shifting to what you really want, despite what it looks like. When we fight and argue, we are only acting out our secret wishes to be something other than what God created us to be. The Holy Spirit won't fail in His job to replace what we have made of our relationship. We do want to remember that since there is only one of us, whatever we choose to perceive about our partners is how we perceive ourselves.

Perhaps it's time for another joke to lighten the mood: A woman goes to the doctor and tells him her husband is losing interest in sex. So the doctor gives her a pill, but warns her that it's still experimental. He says she should slip it into his food at dinner, so that evening, she does just that. About a week later, she goes back to the doctor for her follow-up appointment. She says, "Doc, that pill you gave me worked great! I hid it in his food just like you said! It wasn't five minutes later that he jumped up, pushed all the food and dishes onto the floor, grabbed me, ripped all my clothes off, and ravaged me right there on the table!" The doctor, a little taken aback, says, "I'm sorry, we didn't realize the pill was that strong! The foundation will be glad to pay for any damages." The woman says, "Nah, that's okay. We're never going back to that restaurant anyway."

Humor helps us stay focused on a reality beyond the veil of forgetfulness. It's this reality that says, "Nothing is so serious that it cannot be healed." Whenever you are struck with fear, and the feeling of sweat pours down your face when you even think of addressing an issue with your partner, know you are not alone in this feeling, as many people experience it. However, the feeling reinforces the belief you are alone, because your mind's belief has made some things more real or harder to overcome than others. What is required is having faith that it is not you (yourself) that heals, but the power of God or love. There is a line in the Course that is often quoted that says, *There is no order of difficulty in miracles. One is not "harder" or "bigger" than another.*[7] This is what Jesus means:

When you maintain that there must be an order of difficulty in miracles, all you mean is that there are some things you would withhold from truth. You believe truth cannot deal with them only because you would keep them from truth. Very simply, your lack of faith in the power that heals all pain arises from your wish to retain some aspects of reality for fantasy. If you but realized what this must do to your appreciation of the whole! What you reserve for yourself, you take away from Him Who would release you. Unless you give it back, it is inevitable that your perspective on reality be warped and uncorrected.[8]

You are perfectly capable of allowing the power of God to flow through you to solve all problems, because the Holy Spirit (the Voice for God) sees all problems as the same. Not one is harder or bigger to overcome than another. It is only your belief that says otherwise. Do you see how much power you have? The light within you is too big to fail. Jesus is saying we all have the same power He did to transform all darkness and despair into pure truth. Do we want it above all else? That is the "million dollar question." Whether you want it now or later, your innocence remains, but as the Course says, *Why wait for Heaven? Those who seek the light are merely covering their eyes. The light is in them now.*[9] No matter how difficult things may seem in your relationships, or how fearful your attempts to communicate may be, it doesn't mean you aren't already in the light. Jesus further explains, *This light can not be lost. Why wait to find it in the future, or believe it has been lost already, or was never there? It can so easily be looked upon that arguments which prove it is not there become ridiculous.*[10] He doesn't mean arguments with people, but that our egos argue with the truth. The ego has to defend its "reality" by putting up defenses and trying to prove the light has gone. This is what is silly and ridiculous.

My intention for this chapter is that you start to gain some sense of empowerment over your circumstances; that you start to suspect you are not guilty, and therefore, there is no need to be fearful. At first, there is always fear when the separation feels real. We all experience this. The more we keep reinforcing the idea that we are not weak, but strong; not helpless, but all-powerful, then we can experience ourselves as God created us and feel the fullness of the joy and peace that is our natural inheritance.

SAYINGS FROM WILLIAM SHAKESPEARE

As we move into our final chapter, deepening our understanding of ourselves as one in God, I'd like to close this chapter with a few sayings from William Shakespeare, which at this point on our journey, need no explanation:

> "We are such stuff as dreams are made on, and our little life is rounded with a sleep."

> "God hath given you one face, and you make yourselves another."

> "It is neither good nor bad, but thinking makes it so."

> "Life…is a tale told by an idiot, full of sound and fury, signifying nothing."

> "Nothing can come of nothing."

> "The robbed that smiles, steals something from the thief."

> "Love sought is good, but given unsought, is better."

PAGE FOR PERSONAL NOTES

CHAPTER 13

THE ULTIMATE RELATIONSHIP

*And let Him Whose teaching is only of God teach you the only
meaning of relationships. For God created the only relationship that
has meaning, and that is His relationship with you.*[1]

W e have now come to our closing chapter, which culminates
with the understanding that everything is meaningless that
does not have love as its foundation. Jesus says, *When the Atonement
has been completed, all talents will be shared by all the Sons of God. God is
not partial. All His children have His total Love, and all His gifts are freely
given to everyone alike. "Except ye become as little children" means that
unless you fully recognize your complete dependence on God, you cannot
know the real power of the Son in his true relationship with the Father. The
specialness of God's Sons does not stem from exclusion but from inclusion.
All my brothers are special. If they believe they are deprived of anything,
their perception becomes distorted. When this occurs the whole family of
God, or the Sonship, is impaired in its relationships.*[2]

It is the belief in lack and unworthiness that keeps us all on the
lower rungs of the ladder and blocks our progress towards enlightenment. Now is the time; the time to claim our natural inheritance,

which heals all impaired relationships. Recognizing God as our only Source, we can truly understand the difference between what is meaningful and what is meaningless. In order to awaken to the ultimate relationship, that which you have with God, it is helpful to review how you can use your special relationships, which can be transformed into holy relationships, as a prerequisite to awakening in God. To transform your special relationships into holy relationships, it is necessary to give them over to the Holy Spirit to be used for healing, as a classroom for forgiveness. To do this requires the awareness that when an opportunity arises to meet attack, you respond with love. It is in this kind of willingness to see things differently, that you will notice progress.

A DOWNLOAD FROM SPIRIT

In the face of challenges, it is important to remember that there are only two forms of expression; either someone is expressing love or calling out for love. The response to both of these would be love. This is seldom easy, but if you want peace above all else, you will learn to apply love to any situation or person. In order to use your special relationships to your advantage, practice seeing every challenge as a blessing, in that it enables you to practice seeing the face of Christ in your partner, others, and yourself. In relation to this, one day while Gary and I were presenting our online class, I received what I call a "download" from Spirit. It felt like Jesus's presence was speaking through me, because I didn't have to think at all about what I was saying. The words just spoke through me with no effort at all on my part. For the next few moments I seemed to slip into a trance as the following words were expressed through me:

Jesus appears to each of us every day if we look for Him in all our brothers and sisters. If we look for the face of Christ in everyone, that is what the Holy Spirit wants us to do; what the Holy Spirit is getting all of us to see. The Holy Spirt is appearing to us all the time through our brothers and *sisters if that's what we **choose** to see, because we are all the same; we are all the Christ with Jesus. He would not want us to put Him on a pedestal. He's a wise elder brother, and yes, it's wise to listen to a wise elder brother, but we find Him in everyone if that's what we **want** to see. Until we want that above all else, he says, we will default to the ego's version of the story about someone. We will default to seeing images as reality until we change our minds and remember that there is no difference between us and Jesus, except in time, he says, but time's not real. That is the ultimate understanding, to get to the place where we truly know we're not separate from Him or from God. See Him in everybody. Treat everyone as if He were right in front of you; the same as if they were Jesus, because that's reality. That's the truth. None of us are different from Him or from God. It's only when we choose illusions, or choose to make images more important than what is beyond the veil, that we suffer. It's not always easy. It's not easy to do it all the time, but we can get really good at this with continued practice.*

*The Course is a big teaching. No doubt many of you have the following experience: Doesn't it feel sometimes, that when you continue reading the Course, you keep getting it at deeper and deeper levels, even if you have read a certain passage a hundred times? When you experience that, you exclaim, "Oh my God!" because it just clicks, as if you just got it for the first time, even though you've read it a hundred times. It's because you're getting it, and your mind is being healed, because the more you're forgiving and loving, and you're **living** the Course, the more it's going to be your experience. You're going to feel lighter, like you are dreaming the dream; that you're just walking through the dream, but you're not a figure in the dream. That's the experience the Course is directing us towards; this lightness, this feeling that this is really a dream. It might happen and you feel it for just a few seconds, and then it just goes away, like revelation. It might just be a few seconds and you go "Oh my God, Oh my God, I just had the most awesome feeling!" And in that moment, everything is perfect; all suspension of doubt and fear; and there is nothing in the world that can compare to it; nothing. That's similar to being in direct communion with God, but you can't explain it. You just* *know you want that more than anything, because you're remembering that that's who you are. You're that complete truth, wholeness and oneness with God's love. This world cannot compare to that. Love in this world cannot compare to that, meaning our special love relationships are not at all like the love of God. So, the Course is really deep, and the deeper you go into it, the deeper it goes into **you**, and you will experience these truths.*

After this download, I felt so inspired, and felt total gratitude for the reminder that the more we practice, the more we will all keep making progress.

HOLY RELATIONSHIPS IN HISTORY

I thought it would be helpful to take some examples of relationships and people in history who have actually demonstrated the transformation of a special relationship into a holy one; ones that demonstrated unconditional love, commitment, wisdom, and courage in the face of adversity.

One of the most inspiring and well-known romantic relationships in literary history is that of Elizabeth Barrett Browning and Robert Browning; both poets in the Victorian era. The love affair between Robert Browning and Elizabeth Barrett Browning was one of true passion. It appeared that Elizabeth suffered a severe spinal injury at a young age, causing her to be confined to bed. During this time, she began to write poetry, which started as a hobby when she was around thirteen years old. In 1844, she published her first complete book entitled Poems. Her work caught the attention of Robert Browning. He contacted Elizabeth, and they began a courtship by mail. He contacted her to express his admiration for her, and their affair began with a series of love letters, which captured the intensity of their relationship. As Frederic Kenyon writes, "Mr. Browning knew that he was asking to be allowed to take charge of an invalid's life—believed indeed that she was even worse than was really the case, and that she was hopelessly incapacitated from ever standing on her feet—-but was sure enough of his love to regard that as no obstacle." This is an important point. He didn't let what might be considered an obstacle get in the way of his love and feelings for Elizabeth, which reminds me of the following line from the Course, which you can say with the Holy Spirit's help regarding any challenging situation: *Teach me how **not** to make of it an obstacle to peace, but let You use it for me, to facilitate its coming.*[3]

They later got married, which was kept a secret. Elizabeth's father disapproved of the marriage and wouldn't have anything to do with her after that point. Elizabeth stood by her husband regardless of her father's opinion (another powerful lesson) and she credited him for saving her life. She is quoted as saying, "I admire such qualities as he has—fortitude, integrity. I loved him for his courage in adverse circumstances which were yet felt by him more literally than I could feel them."

During their early years of marriage, there were many poetic expressions in the form of sonnets, which Robert Browning preserved. "I dared not," he said, "reserve to myself the finest sonnets written in any language since Shakespeare's." The collection finally appeared in 1850 as "Sonnets from the Portuguese." Kenyon writes, "With the single exception of Rossetti, no modern English poet has written of love with such genius, such beauty, and such sincerity, as the two who gave the most beautiful example of it in their own lives."

Note: What strikes me is the overwhelming sincerity of their love, and its rising above adversity. Elizabeth died in Robert's arms on June 29, 1861. The following quote was taken from an internet source on her love for Robert:

"Sonnet 43, one of Barrett's poems, expresses Barrett's intense love for her husband-to-be, Robert Browning. So intense is her love for him, she says, that it rises to the spiritual level. She loves him freely, without coercion; she loves him purely, without expectation of personal gain. She even loves him with an intensity of the suffering resembling that of Christ on the cross, and she loves him in the way that she loved saints as a child. Moreover, she expects to continue to love him after death."

Note: The reference to Christ suffering is really about her own intense, unconditional love for her husband. Christ didn't really suffer on the cross as the guiltless mind can't suffer, and Jesus knew this. The reference to saints here could be those personal people in her life growing up whom she considered saints, yet they disappointed her, but it didn't stop her from experiencing the purity of love in her life. To me, her story of their love through one of her most famous sonnets, describes her complete and unconditional devotion to love without limits.

The term "Sonnet" is derived from Sonnetto, meaning "little song." The sonnet is worthy of reviewing here:

How do I love thee? Let me count the ways.

I love thee to the depth and breadth and height my soul can reach, when feeling out of sight, for the ends of being and ideal Grace. I love thee to the level of everyday's most quiet need, by sun and candle-light.

I love thee freely, as men strive for Right;

I love thee purely, as they turn from Praise.

I love thee with the passion put to use in my old griefs, and with my childhood's faith.

I love thee with a love I seemed to lose with my lost saints!---I love thee with the breath, smiles, tears, of all my life!---and, if God choose, I shall but love thee better after death…

Note: I was so moved by these words that I wrote a melody to them, which can be found on my CD, *Awakening to Love.*

I was also guided by Spirit to a particular story about Queen Esther in the *Old Testament Book of Esther* having to do with devotion, courage, and faith, which I believe is worthy of sharing. It has been said that courage is not the absence of fear, but the mastery of it. The story of Esther, the Queen of the Persian Empire, certainly captures this very important theme, and is a prime example of character traits such as devotion, faith, grace, and trust in a power greater than oneself; developing one's relationship with God, the ultimate relationship. All of us from time to time slip into trusting in the weakness of the ego as our strength. If we remember to join with the Holy Spirit, and place our trust in Him to do the work through us, we are better vessels for love to flow through us, which is the Holy Spirit's purpose for the body, and the purpose of relationships.

In the story of Esther, she was born without a mother or father, so she was born with the idea that she belonged to no one. She would later use her feelings of isolation and loneliness as tools to allow her to find her Spirit in her experiences. You can do this, too, by remembering to see others with spiritual sight. Think of people being nothing less than God, which means *you* are nothing less than God. In other words, we can learn to find our Spirit in times of challenge instead of losing ourselves. Esther's devotion to God was formed as a result of her feelings of emptiness and isolation. She used these feelings for a different purpose, as inspiration to connect with God, her one and only parent (the ultimate relationship).

Esther had the ability to see through the walls of separation and find God. Our relationship with God can often feel deceptive because of the seeming separation we feel from Him. In other words, we don't always experience an immediate reaction when we call on Him. But notice that we are not beaten down by God when we veer off the path by making mistaken choices with the ego. God only knows our wholeness.

Just the same, when we look within and find our answers there, and as we practice forgiveness, we don't always experience material gains or even better health. Things still seem to go on as they were before. The world may not change, but our mind about the world will change as we practice forgiveness. We will always see suffering until we are willing to go beyond where we are now in our minds and move through the blocks that keep us from experiencing love's presence. Esther was a master at moving beyond the blocks that appeared to surround her. She apparently taught herself this and used her more challenging years for this purpose. She learned to see God everywhere, as if she knew He was her only parent. He was the only Authority. **In truth, there is no veil between God and His Son (all of us as one), so there is no relationship in that sense. God is one continuous stream of love, extending Itself into eternity, and we are part of that love.**

All of us have times when we are challenged; times when the ego's voice is much louder than the Holy Spirit's voice. The ego usually speaks first when we let it, and is the loudest. Instead of allowing the ego to lead us further into temptation, we can choose to see ourselves climbing back up the ladder the ego led us down, but now with the Holy Spirit as our teacher. Step by step, thought by thought, we undo the ego, and eventually we will reach the top of the ladder. This is the *period of achievement*[4] the Course talks about in the *Development of Trust*,[5] where we have learned to trust only the Voice of the Holy Spirit as our teacher.

Esther exhibited these traits even with the possibility of losing her own life, which would end up saving many others. The story of Esther shows a person who was Christ-like in her selflessness, willing to give up her own life for the sake of all. This wouldn't have been sacrificial, but rather a heroic attempt to save her own people (the Jews) from being destroyed by the King.

This story demonstrates the blessings that come upon those who are devoted and have complete trust in God. In my opinion, Esther demonstrated that her relationship with God was most important. This is what we are all working towards, healing our unconscious guilt over believing we've separated from our Creator. Our special relationships with others are beautiful opportunities to practice this mindset, if we wisely use them for this purpose.

Jesus and his beloved wife, Mary Magdalene, are another example of such a partnership, where devotion to the truth and to God through their holy relationship with each other was most apparent. They were equals as teachers, and Mary also had a following. They were "normal" in the sense that that they didn't act as if they were above everyone else. They were simply messengers of the truth, teaching through joining rather than separating from society. They were married, and I would call their relationship one of spiritual partnership or a holy relationship. They certainly demonstrated what it means to have a holy relationship, which is a stage you reach in a relationship where growing spiritually as a couple for the purpose of awakening together as *one in God* becomes the ultimate goal of the relationship.

In the old paradigm of marriage, the purpose seems to be more about survival in the relationship and what each person can get from the other to complete each other. This fulfills the ego's need for specialness. Spiritual partnership is more about understanding that you are both already whole, and you are joining together because you recognize the value of what you can share with each other and others, which prepares you for awakening to your true relationship with your Creator, the *ultimate relationship, where you recognize your oneness.*

I'll never forget the last scene in the film, "Pompeii," starring Kit Harington and Emily Browning. In this final scene when Vesuvius was erupting, the two stars were frantically trying to escape along with everyone else. It was obvious that the eruption was going to consume absolutely everything in its path, and these two lovers knew it. Finally, the woman stops and looks at the man and says "I don't want to spend my last moments running." He looks at her as the volcanic storm is coming directly towards them at incredible speed, and says, "Don't look there, look at me...just look at me." Instead of focusing on the chaos, they spent their last moments sharing a passionate kiss, only looking directly into each other's eyes. You see this as the horrific image of the storm is almost upon them. It's very dramatic, but shows duality in action. This intensely moving scene is also highly symbolic of choosing love over fear even in the face of your imminent death.

Despite all the drama that plays out in our lives, we can still choose to live a gentle, happy dream of forgiveness, which precedes the awakening to our true home in Heaven. Cultivating a holy relationship with someone precedes the developing awareness of your true relationship with God. To develop your relationship with God is to spend a period of time each day devoted to Him. Take a few moments each day and think about God. Exercising True Prayer as discussed in the Song of Prayer supplement of the Course is one of the tools you can use to join with God and develop your relationship with Him. In True Prayer, you forget the things you think you need, and go with empty hands unto your Father. You have no idols to worship before him. Let them all go. Ask only that you understand that you have been given everything.

I often ponder how much time most of us spend in a day on our routines and habits, kind of like robots walking around on automatic pilot, completely caught up in the world and our stories. There is no need for guilt, because it didn't really happen in reality. Since we believe it happened there is work to be done to undo it. We have over-learned the ego to such an extent that it takes quite a bit of undoing to even begin to recognize how little time we spend on spiritual pursuits and joining with God. There is great resistance to doing this, because it feels threatening to the ego, so we might find ourselves saying, "It takes too much work!" We say it takes a lot of work, yet we are willing to go to work every day and spend hours and hours doing things most of us don't want to do. Strange indeed! Eventually when we value Spirit more, all of us in our own time will choose to develop our relationship with God and remember who we are; a part of Him, Whom He created to be exactly the same as He is.

A METAPHOR FOR
UNDERSTANDING THE TRUTH

The Sun is like a metaphor for who we all really are: The Light of the World that lightens *up* the world! In the Course, light means truth. In the following metaphor, the Sun, as we experience it here on Earth, is a constant in the sense that it consistently shines.   We know that its shining brilliance is something we can always count on. The Sun is the source of all life on the level of form (in the physical world) because we *believe* that it sustains us, just as God is the Source of all life, period. The clouds that obscure the Sun from time to time are like a metaphor for the unconscious guilt in our minds, obscuring the truth of who we are as a part of God. Just as we know that the clouds only obscure the Sun temporarily, our unconscious guilt also obscures the truth of who we are temporarily. It doesn't change the truth, just as the clouds obscuring the sun don't change the fact that the sun always shines. We don't condemn or get angry at the clouds for coming out because we know that it is only a block to the Sun's presence, and that the Sun will continue shining above the clouds. The Sun remains unaffected by what is outside of it.

In truth, as is everything else in this illusory world, the Sun is just an image that we made, and it will disappear into oneness with everything else in the false universe. **At the level of the world where we believe we are, we know that it would be silly to start yelling and getting angry at the clouds for coming out and blocking the Sun. We just accept the clouds because we know the Sun always shines beyond it. So, if the people in our lives are also projections coming from our unconscious mind, why do we condemn and blame others when they block the light from *their* minds?**

You can learn to accept that the people that push your buttons or annoy you are only experiencing temporary blocks in accepting the love within them. If you react to them with your ego, then you are also blocking the love within yourself as well. You can develop your relationship with God by practicing within your special relationships. That's what they are for; for forgiveness. Eventually, you will attain the goal of the Course and experience your Divine nature through the understanding that *Enlightenment is but a recognition, not a change at all. Light is not of the world, yet you who bear the light in you are alien here as well. The light came with you from your native home, and stayed with you because it is your own. It is the only thing you bring with you from Him Who is your Source. It shines in you because it lights your home, and leads you back to where it came from and you are at home.*[6]

All the while, in the story of our lives, the Sun still shines, just as the truth is still the truth, and doesn't shift or change, and the truth is … **God Is.**

PAGE FOR PERSONAL NOTES

ABOUT THE AUTHOR

Cindy Lora-Renard is an international speaker on *A Course in Miracles*, and the author of *A Course in Health and Well-Being* (published in six languages) and the best-selling books, *The Business of Forgiveness* and *Heaven is Now*. Cindy and her husband, Gary Renard, also facilitate two 2-hour online classes on *A Course in Miracles* every month. In addition, Cindy has a Master's degree in Spiritual Psychology from the University of Santa Monica, and is also a visionary singer and songwriter. She uses her knowledge of *A Course in Miracles*, music, and psychology, as healing tools to help others awaken from the dream of separation to the higher octaves of life.

Cindy was born in Toledo, Ohio, to two very educated and accomplished teachers. Her father, Ron Lora (now in retirement) is an award-winning History Professor who taught at the University of Toledo in Ohio. Her mother, Doris Lora (now in retirement) was a highly respected Music Professor at the same University, who later changed careers and received her Ph.D. in Psychology. Both continue to remain very active in their communities. When Cindy was 17 she moved out to Los Angeles, California with her mother where she still resides. She started on a spiritual path in her early 20's, going through the spiritual buffet line until she encountered *A Course in Miracles*, which became her chosen path. She eventually met and fell in love with her husband, Gary Renard, also a prominent teacher of *A Course in Miracles*, and best-selling author of several books of his own. A gradual process unfolded where Cindy realized the direction her path was meant to take. She continues to enjoy her work as a writer, speaker, and facilitator of online classes with Gary, and presenting audio recordings on *A Course in Miracles* through her website. She loves to meet people from around the world. She likes to say, "We are all in this together."

KEY TO REFERENCES

As a key to footnotes and references, please follow the examples below of the numbering system used for A Course in Miracles. Other resources quoted from are also noted below.

T-26.IV.4:7. = Text, Chapter 26, Section IV, Paragraph 4, Sentence 7.

W-p1.169.5:2. = Workbook, Part 1, Lesson 169, Paragraph 5, Sentence 2.

M-13.3:2. = Manual, Question 13, Paragraph 3, Sentence 2.

C-6.4:6 = Clarification of Terms, Term 6, Paragraph 4, Sentence 6.

P-2.VI.5:1. = Psychotherapy, Chapter 2, Section 6, Paragraph 5, Sentence 1.

S-1.V.4:3. = Song of Prayer, Chapter 1, Section 5, Paragraph 4, Sentence 3.

In. = Intro.

YIR.Ch.2.P. 9 = Your Immortal Reality: How to Break the Cycle of Birth and Death by Gary. R. Renard, Chapter 2, Page 9

DU.Ch.4.P.365 = The Disappearance of the Universe by Gary R. Renard, Chapter 4, Page 365

LHFNO = Love Has Forgotten No One by Gary R. Renard

Preface of ACIM = Preface of A Course in Miracles

ENDNOTES

1. **The Purpose of Relationships**   1. P-1.2:1 2. T-9.VII.1:6-7
3. T-21.in.1:5 4. M-20.4:8   5. T-20.VIII.1:2 6. T-9.VII.3:7-8 7.
M-3.1:6-8 8. T-8.III.4:2-5 9. T-22.VI.14:5 10. T-17.VI.2:3 11. T-19.I
12. T-19.I.1:1 13. T-19.I.1:3 14. T-19.II.1:1-6 15. T-19.II.2:1-4 16.
T-19.II.6:7-8 17. T-31.VIII.9:2 18. T-19.I.9:1-5 19. T-21.in.1:1-5
20. M-in.2:1-3

2. **The Power of the Present** 1. T-15.I.10:1 2. T-15.I.9:2-3 3. T-15.I.9:5
4. T-15.II.6:3 5. YIR.Ch.3.P.80 6. DU.Ch.7.P.256 7. T-19.IV-C.5:6
8. W-p1.185.1:1-2 9. T-18.VII.7:7-8 10. T-18.VII.8:4 11. T-in.2:2-
3 12. T-6.I.18:1-2 13. Preface,What it Says,p.xii 14. M-17.4:1-11
15. T-15.I.8:1-7 16. T-28.I 17. T-28.I.4:4-7 18. T-28.I.7:3-9 19.
T-9.V.6:3-5 20. T-15.I.9:3-7 21. T-15.V.3:1-7

3. **Adventures in Traveling.** 1. T-16.VII.4:1-3 2. T-7.VIII.3:9-12 3.
W-201 4. T-5.V.5:1 5. T-18.IV.2:1-2 6. T-18.IV.2:1-4 7. www.acim.
org

4. **The Tools.** 1. T-1.II.6;7 2. W-in.1:3 3. T-1.I.43:1 4. DU.Ch.2.P.39
5. S-2.II 6. W-23.5:2   7. YIR.Ch.3.P.78 8. YIR.Ch.3.P.80 9.
W-121.10-13 10. T-23.IV 11. W-185.6:1-2 12. W-132.5:3 13. T-9.
IV.5:3-6 14. T-31.VI.2:1-7 15. T-2.II.1:11-12 16. T-2.II.1:9 17. T-9.
VII.8:1-3

5. **Perception is Interpretation.** 1. T-1.III.6:7 2. T-14.XI.5:1-2 3. T-23.II.22:8-11 4. T-21.IV.3:1 5. Preface.6:3-9 6. T-30.I 7. T-18. II.5:12-15 8. T-27.VII.11:7 9. T-27.VII.8:1 10. T-10.I.2:1 11. T-5. IV.4:5-6 12. T-3.V.9:1 13. T-3.III.2:1-4:6 14. T-27.VIII.6:2-4 15. T-1.I.1:1

6. **Infidelity.** 1. T-31.VIII.1:1-2 2. M-4 3. M-4.II.1:4-9 4. T-29. IV.4:1-3 5. T-29.IV.6:1-4 6. Preface.2:2-9 7. T-1.III.6:1-7 8. T-4. IV.8:1-10

7. **Abundance is a State of Mind.** 1. T-9.VIII.5:1 2. T-1.V.6:2-3 3. T-7.IV.7:1 4. W-166.9:2 5. W-166.9:1-6 6. T-26.X.4;1 7. T-27.I.1:5-9 8. T-18.I.4:1-6 9. T-15.I.10:7-8 10. W-289

8. **Reality as Co-Creating with God.** 1. T-25.VII.4:2-3 2. T-4. III.1:10 3. T-in.1:1-8 4. T-4.IV.8;1-6 5. W-169.5:1-7

9. **The Right-Minded Relationship.** 1. C-1.5:2 2. TW-132 3. W-132.4:1-5:3 4. W-132.7:1-4 5. T-5.IV.8:1-6 6. T-15.I.11:1-2 7. T-3.IV.2:3 8. T-27.I 9. T-27.VIII 10. T-27.VIII.10:1-6 11. T-27. VIII.11:1-2 12. T-31.VIII.11:1 13. M-14.1:2-5 14. T-23.IV 15. T-16. VI.10:1-2

10. **Happy or Right.** 1. T-29.VII.1:6-9 2. T-30.I.2:2 3. T-30.I.4:2 4. M-21.I:9-10 5. T-8.III.4:2-6 6. W-pII.I.1:1-7 7. T-27.VIII.4:4-5 8. C-1.1:1 9.Let it Be, song and lyrics by Paul McCartney

11. **Isn't That Special?** 1. T-16.VII.4:1 2. M-4.VIII.1:1-3 3. T-16. IV.3:1-7 4. T-1.VI.5:4-10 5. M-3.1:6-8 6. W-195.1:1-6 7. T-15.V.3:1-7 8. T-15.V.4:1-6 9. W-134.15:3 10. W-134.16:3-4

12. **Fearless Communication.** 1. T-15.IX.7:1 2. T-5.V.5:1 3. T-31. VIII.5:2-4 4. M-10.2:1-7 5. T-6.in.1:2-3 6. T-18.V.6:1-3 7. T-1.I.1:1-3 8. T-17.I.3:1-6 9. W-188.1:1-3 10. W-188.2:1-3

13. **The Ultimate Relationship.** 1. T-15.VIII.6:5-6 2. T-1.V.3:1-8 3. T-19.IV-C.11:10 4. M-4.I-A.8:1 5. M-4.I-A 6. W-188.1:4-8

SUGGESTED READINGS AND RESOURCES ON A COURSE IN MIRACLES

1. "A Course in Miracles," 3rd Edition, published by The Foundation for Inner Peace

2. "The Disappearance of the Universe" by Gary R. Renard

3. "Your Immortal Reality: How to Break the Cycle of Birth and Death" by Gary R. Renard

4. "Love Has Forgotten No One" by Gary R. Renard

5. "The Lifetimes When Jesus and Buddha Knew Each Other: A History of Mighty Companions" by Gary R. Renard

6. "A Course in Health and Well-Being" by Cindy Lora-Renard

7. "The Business of Forgiveness" by Cindy Lora-Renard

8. "Heaven is Now" by Cindy Lora-Renard

9. "All Peace, No Pieces" by Jackie Lora-Jones

10. "The Most Commonly Asked Questions About A Course in Miracles" by Gloria and Kenneth Wapnick, Ph.D.

11. "Absence From Felicity" by Kenneth Wapnick, Ph.D

12. "Healing the Unhealed Mind" by Kenneth Wapnick, Ph.D.

13. "A Vast Illusion" by Kenneth Wapnick, Ph.D

14. "Journey without Distance" by Robert Skutch

15. Online classes with Gary and Cindy Renard on A Course in Miracles:

To subscribe to the classes, please go to the Appearances page at www.cindylora.com

You will also find a list of products at Cindy's Store page on her website, including newly released audio recordings (for digital download) on A Course in Miracles.

Spiritual Coupling

Other books and Products by Cindy Lora-Renard:

A Course in Health and Well-Being

The Business of Forgiveness

Heaven is Now

Music and Meditation CD's, which can be found
on Amazon, iTunes, and CD baby:

Journey through Sound

Awakening to Love

Near the Beginning

Summer and Smoke

Meditations for Couples

Downloadable Audio Recordings on A Course in Miracles
at the Store page of Cindy's website:

www.cindylora.com

THE FOUNDATION
FOR INNER PEACE

To learn more about A Course in Miracles, I recommend you visit the website of the authorized publisher and copyright holder of the Course, the Foundation for Inner Peace: www.acim.org. While there are many excellent organizations supporting study of A Course in Miracles, this is the original one with the greatest variety and depth of Course-related materials, including biographies and photos of the scribes, DVDs, free access to daily Lessons, audio recordings, information about the many languages into which the Course has been translated, and electronic versions of the Course, including mobile device apps.

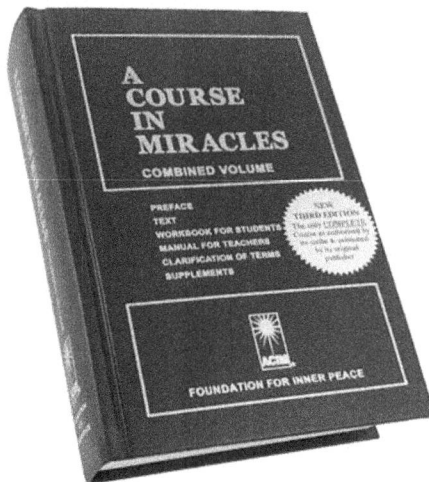

The Foundation for Inner Peace is a non-profit organization dedicated to uplifting humanity through A Course in Miracles. The organization depends on donations and is currently immersed in translating the Course into many languages (26 to date). The Foundation also donates thousands of copies of the Course. If you would like to make it possible for more people to benefit from A Course in Miracles, please donate to the Foundation for Inner Peace or one of the many other fine Course-related organizations.

www.ingramcontent.com/pod-product-compliance
Lightning Source LLC
Chambersburg PA
CBHW052033090426
42739CB00010B/1888